Managing
Bipolar Affective Disorder

G Sachs
Massachusetts General Hospital and
Harvard Medical School

SP
SCIENCE
PRESS ■

Published by Science Press Ltd, Porters South, 4 Crinan Street, London N1 9XW, UK.

© 2004 Science Press Ltd

http://www.science-press.com/

British Library Cataloguing in Publication Data.

A catalogue record for this book is available from the British Library.

ISBN 1 85873 838 5

Project editor: Jenny Collins
Project manager: Maria Antoniou
Illustrator: Matthew McCutcheon
Designer: Simon Banister
Production: Laurent Lafon

Printed in the USA by IPC

Contents

Author biography

Gary S Sachs MD is Director of the Bipolar Mood Disorder Clinic and Director of the Harvard Bipolar Research Program at Massachusetts General Hospital (MGH) in Boston, Massachusetts and Associate Professor of Psychiatry at Harvard Medical School.

His experience with bipolar disorder began in 1970 on his first day as a volunteer at a state mental hospital outside Baltimore, Maryland. Walking on to the ward for the first time left him with lasting impressions of both the frightful behavior exhibited by some psychotic and excited patients and the therapeutic optimism expressed by staff awaiting a soon to be available new treatment. This opportunity to witness firsthand the dramatic improvements that followed the introduction of lithium was a powerful influence on the decision leading to his career work being focused on bipolar disorder and its treatment.

After graduating from the University of Pennsylvania in 1976, he gained research experience in experimental psychology at Cambridge University. A 1982 graduate of the University of Maryland School of Medicine, he completed his residency in psychiatry at Massachusetts General Hospital. There he served as Chief Resident of the Acute Psychiatry Service, Clinical Fellow in Psychiatry, and Director of Chronobiology Section in the Clinical Psychopharmacology Unit at MGH, before founding the Bipolar Research Program and Clinic in 1988. Among his many achievements, Dr. Sachs has received a Thouron Scholarship from the University of Pennsylvania, the Dupont-Warren Fellowship from the Harvard Medical School, and the Dunlop Award for his achievements in psychiatric research and writing.

Dr Sachs' academic work, numbering more than 100 publications, is focused primarily on improving understanding and treatment of bipolar disorder. He has been actively involved in the formulation of several national and international treatment guidelines for bipolar disorder. He is co-editor-in-chief of *Clinical Approaches in Bipolar Disorder* and on the review board of several leading journals. In addition, Dr Sachs is a member of the American Psychiatric Association and the International Society for Bipolar Disorder. He serves on national advisory boards for the Depression and Bipolar Support Alliance (DBSA) and the National Alliance for the Mentally Ill (NAMI).

Dr Sachs is principal investigator for the National Institute of Mental Health (NIMH)-sponsored Systematic Treatment Enhancement Program for Bipolar Disorder (STEP-BD). This project includes the largest NIMH clinical studies conducted to date. In addition to several clinical trials examining medication and psychosocial interventions, STEP-BD conducts genetics research, women's health studies and a disease management program that emphasize continuity of care for all people with bipolar disorder.

Dedication

This book is dedicated to my wife Maryanne whose inexhaustible advice, support, patience, and understanding transforms book writing and many other daunting projects from improbable dreams into attainable realities.

Preface

Over the past century, accumulation of evidence has advanced the diagnosis and treatment of mood disorders dramatically. In his seminal work, Kraepelin used age of onset and course of illness data to distinguish what he termed manic-depressive insanity from many conditions with overlapping cross-sectional phenomenology. Giving precedence to longitudinal data, Dr Kraepelin recognized the similarities of various forms of affective illness and thereby established the modern concept of mood disorders. The Diagnostic and Statistical Manual (DSM) IV classification of mood disorders – informed by evidence from epidemiology, family studies, clinical trials, and reliability testing – recognizes unipolar and bipolar forms of mood disorder and conceptualizes further distinct subtypes within each category.

Cade's 1949 report of the calming effect of lithium spawned a half-century of progress which transformed basic aspects of psychiatric practice. Acceptance of lithium as a therapeutic agent required the invention of the randomized controlled trial; this new technology made it clear that psychiatric illness was amenable to medical treatment. The science of clinical research also necessitated increased diagnostic rigor. Development of operational diagnostic criteria and reliable assessment techniques such as the Present State Exam, Schedule for Affective Disorders and Schizophrenia (SADS), and the Structured Clinical Interview for DSM (SCID), along with standardized scales for rating symptom severity, has resulted in the indispensable instrumentation of the clinical research laboratory. Reliable assessments bulwark the evidence-based approach to psychiatric practice against persistent antagonists who prefer to mythologize mental illness.

Evidence has driven the evolution of the definition of manic depressive illness in a direction counter to the preference of most clinical scientists, from an imprecise but narrowly defined condition into the DSM-IV's operationally defined but more inclusive unipolar and bipolar mood disorders [1]. The twenty-first century opens with this nosological paradox and a parallel clinical paradox: even as clinical efficacy studies expand the armamentarium of evidence-based treatments, the population of bipolar patients with inadequate response to these treatments seems to grow ever larger [2].

This manual consists of basic information about bipolar illness, guidelines for a systematic disease management program, and practical information related to the treatments described in the pathways. The disease management program offered in this book is intended to cope with the challenges and potential pitfalls that stem from this frustrating reality in several ways.

First, standardizing the assessment and systematizing the overall management of patients facilitates the accumulation of a meaningful record of outcomes for each treatment intervention made. This class of evidence, the reliably assessed outcome of treatment, seems likely to gain recognition as a critical dimension of diagnostic subtyping and treatment choice. Such recorded individual evidence provides the opportunity for an individualized iterative treatment strategy. As the physicians manage their patients and measure treatment response as they progress along the various pathways covered in this book, records and a systematic approach help to generate progressively better answers to complex clinical questions.

Second, while far from comprehensive, this book offers concise guidance on how to address many of the most common issues that arise during the course of treating bipolar illness. Each of the sections on clinical pathways starts with a mini-review of the current state of evidence and then describes sequences of decision points and recommendations.

Third, the pathways were constructed to systematize rather than constrain clinical decision, and the "menu of reasonable choices" provided at key decision points simply reflects an application of currently available evidence. As each pathway is reviewed, the physician should bear in mind that the goal is to encourage an evidence-based approach in which they will construct a set of recommendations at each decision point rather than rigidly following the recommendations as they are listed here. These pages are set, but the "menu of reasonable choices" should be dynamic, changing as new evidence, new therapies, and new data pertaining to an individual patient become available.

References

1. Greil W, Kleindienst N. **Concepts in the treatment of bipolar disorder.** *Acta Psychiatr Scand Suppl* 2003; **418**:41–46.

2. Frank E, Judge R. **Treatment recommendations versus treatment realities: recognizing the rift and understanding the consequences.** *J Clin Psychiatry* 2001; **62** (suppl 22):10–15.

Chapter 1

Introduction to the
Collaborative Care Model

Bipolar disorder (BD) is a common, potentially deadly disease that can be treated but not cured. Treatment is seldom completely effective, but appropriate treatment can dramatically reduce the disability and excessive mortality associated with bipolar disorder [1,2]. The overarching goal of this book is to provide methods and information that can maximize the beneficial impact of treatment.

Attempts to construct comprehensive algorithms frequently prove counter-productive simply because guidelines that approach the complexity required quickly render a densely detailed algorithm, unsuitable for use by the practising clinician. This book attempts to aid the clinical process by offering suggestions for a disease management model in which sequences of decision points and treatment options are organized into simple pathways.

This chapter introduces general principles of a collaborative care model designed for management of BD, and describes the skills and strategies fundamental to the collaborative management of this:

- weighing evidence;

- clinical assessment;

- education;

- negotiation;

- intervention; and

- the multiphase strategy common to the clinical pathways
  (presented in subsequent chapters).

While each of these skills and strategies can be used alone, the combination provides a disease management model more powerful than the sum of its individual parts. The concepts in this model are broadly applicable to the management of patients with other diagnoses.

BD challenges even the most experienced clinician. Inherent variability of symptoms, high rates of substance abuse, anxiety disorders, medical comorbidity, a substantial risk of suicide, and other potentially severe adverse outcomes are among the characteristics that complicate clinical management of patients with the condition. The desire for guidance created by this apparent chaos spawns many laudable scholarly efforts to construct treatment algorithms and guidelines.

How can the daunting complexity encountered in long-term management of BD be incorporated into a user-friendly model? The collaborative care model presented here does not attempt to be comprehensive (*see* Figure 1.1). Instead it gains

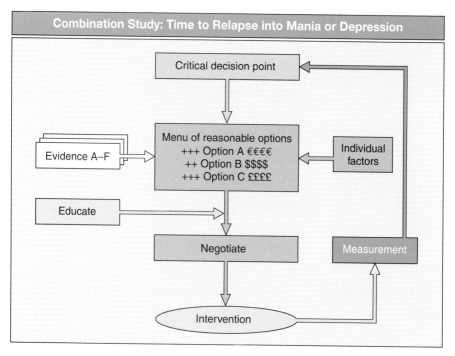

Figure 1.1

utility by offering simple assessment techniques. The pathways described address only the most common decision points in an effort intended to encourage clinicians to adopt the systematic approach to clinical interactions. This includes presenting recommendations for evidence-based treatment options to patients as a menu of reasonable choices.

Assessment

There is no substitute for careful systematic assessment. This process should extend from the initial assessment to every follow-up evaluation and include active listening, probes for specific diagnostic information (including suicidality and substance abuse), and the use of collateral information (from family, friends, medical records, and other care providers). Care providers, patients, and family members share an interest in improving the efficiency of the assessment and intervention process.

Establishing Current and Lifetime Diagnoses

It is important to focus initial neuropsychiatric assessment on accurate determination of lifetime mood disorder diagnosis and current episode; this is critical because these assessments provide the basis for selecting and staging treatment modalities. A complete evaluation includes the patient's psychiatric and medical history, directed physical examination, and indicated laboratories. Routine baseline evaluation should include complete blood count, serum chemistries, and thyroid functions. Electroencephalogram, imaging studies, and erythrocyte sedimentation rate are also reasonable at least once, in order to screen for potential secondary causes of mood episodes.

Bipolar illness is relatively easy to diagnose when the patient presents with a current manic or mixed episode. Failure to diagnose bipolar illness in a depressed patient is a common occurrence and in such cases use of antidepressant medication is frequently associated with treatment-emergent mania. The potential for this unfavorable outcome can be reduced by including systematic screening for episodes of abnormal mood elevation in the evaluation of all patients with mood disorders.

By identifying and characterizing the most extreme period of mood elevation, it is possible to rapidly determine whether a patient meets the criteria for bipolar I, bipolar II, cyclothymia, or bipolar not otherwise specified (NOS) (see Figure 1.2). A template for the standardized affective disorders evaluation used in the Systematic Treatment Enhancement Program for Bipolar Disorder (STEP-BD) can be found on the Harvard Bipolar Program website www.manicdepressive.org [3].

Recording the Diagnosis is Not Enough

Lack of a well-documented episode can cause needless diagnostic revision; this point deserves strong emphasis. The physician's record detailing the most extreme episode, including a narrative and systematic symptoms ratings, often provides the decisive evidence needed to prevent misguided revision of a well-established diagnosis due to poor memory and/or perceptual distortion, both of which accompany abnormal mood episodes.

Avoid Reliance on Self-Report Alone

Mood often colors perception. Since a psychiatrist's direct observation of their patient is usually limited to brief interviews, assessment of bipolar patients can be improved by augmenting the patient's clinical report with reports from significant others. Whenever possible, clinicians should endeavor to establish and maintain a

3

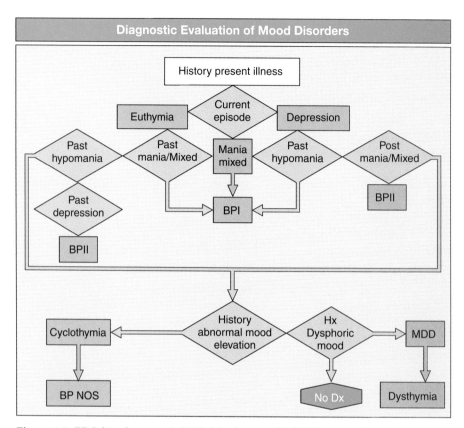

Figure 1.2. BP I, bipolar type I; BP II, bipolar type II; MDD, major depressive disorder; BP NOS, bipolar, not otherwise specified; Hx, history; Dx, diagnosis.

positive therapeutic alliance with the patient, their family, and any systems important in caring for the patient. With the consent of the patient, establishing a policy of open communication gives the psychiatrist access to the important observations of those who know the patient well. Since a central feature of bipolar illness is episodic distortion in self-assessment, this offers the patient some protection against the risk of relying on their self-observation to guide treatment decisions. As the recipient of multiple inputs, the psychiatrist weighs the conflicting descriptions of the patient's symptoms. The sensitivity and specificity of clinical examination is greatly influenced by the illness and the perspective of the reporter. In general, patient self-report is most sensitive and least specific for symptoms of depression. In contrast, friends and family tend to be most sensitive and least specific for symptoms of mood elevation.

Communicating Provisional Diagnostic Impression and Treatment Plan

Once a sufficient fund of information is gathered it can be combined with the clinician's fund of knowledge about psychiatric illness and therapeutics to produce a preliminary diagnostic impression and range of treatment options.

Simply offering a diagnosis and recommending a course of treatment often disadvantages the therapeutic alliance. It is usually more helpful to engage patients by reviewing the facts – the objective evidence as gathered in the assessment – before offering an opinion as to the diagnosis. A diagnostic opinion can be offered forthrightly, while emphasizing the provisional nature of any opinion offered so early in the course of what must be an ongoing assessment process. It is often the case that patients disagree with a diagnostic assessment, but are willing to engage in treatment. Since, in fairness, diagnosis in psychiatry is always subject to revision, it is reasonable to envision response to treatment as part of the assessment process. It is more desirable to be in agreement that a course of treatment has produced results in a patient's interest than it is to persuade the patient to accept a diagnosis.

Using Systematic Follow-up Techniques to Determine Clinical Status at Every Visit

At every follow-up visit, determination of the presence of one of the eight mutually exclusive clinical states listed in Table 1.1 can be linked to a management decision point in one of the clinical pathways. Practitioners accustomed to using the fourth edition of the Diagnostic and Statistical Manual (DSM-IV) will immediately recognize that seven of the eight correspond to familiar terms. The concept of clinical status builds on this familiar nomenclature to improve clinical utility.

Over the course of bipolar illness, patients may present with acute symptoms diagnosable under DSM-IV criteria as fully syndromal episodes of major depression, mania, hypomania, or mixed episodes, or with a "recovered" state (eight weeks with minimal symptomatology). These link easily with clinical pathways but do not suffice to guide treatment over the course of BD.

The DSM-IV designation "partial recovery" is given to two very different groups: patients who remain ill but with symptoms subthreshold for a full episode and euthymic patients whose well state has a duration of less than eight weeks. STEP-BD avoids this management problem by using the separate clinical status designations "continued symptomatic" and "recovering". Therefore, merely by giving separate names to what DSM-IV has already dichotomized we can clearly distinguish ill patients whose fluctuating symptoms are just below the criteria for a full episode from newly well patients.

5

Definitions for Assignment of Clinical Status		
	DSM-IV	**Clinical Status**
Fully Syndromal	Depression Mania Hypomania Mixed	Depression Mania Hypomania Mixed
Subsyndromal	Partial Recovery Symptoms subthreshold for full episode or < eight weeks with minimal symptoms	Continued Symptomatic ≥ 3 moderate symptoms
Well	Recovered	Recovering ≤ 2 moderate symptoms Recovered > eight weeks with ≤ 2 moderate symptoms
New Subsyndromal		Roughening ≥ 3 moderate symptoms following after meeting criteria for recovered

Table 1.1

An eighth term, "roughening", is used to describe the occurrence of new subsyn-dromal symptoms after the patient has met the "recovered" criteria. Roughening indicates an increased likelihood of a new episode [4,5].

Doctor-patient Contact Time is Precious! Use it Efficiently

Even the most skilled clinician often finds their schedule backed up. Many appointments are extended due to inefficient communication. For instance, substantial time expenditure is needed to elicit even simple information such as number of hours slept, or, in the closing minute of an appointment, important information is revealed unexpectedly. Furthermore, after leaving their appointment, patients often experience dismay at having forgotten to tell their care provider something very important. These common frustrations can be reduced by encouraging patients to bring in information recorded outside of appointment time. Patients can participate in their own assessment by completing a waiting room self-report form and a daily mood chart. Examples are available in Appendices 2 and 4 (for downloadable versions *see* www.manicdepressive.org). Active patient collaboration with the assessment routine yields substantial rewards because time efficiency results in more time for unstructured talk with the clinician. In addition, information recorded contemporaneously by the patient at home or in the waiting room improves rapport by providing time-labeled documentation of the patient's subjective experience. This record can be a powerful counter weight when a patient's recollection is colored by nihilism (I've never been well), or euphoric recall (I never had a problem).

With minimal time investment, new patients usually become sufficiently informed to begin contributing as meaningful collaborators to the assessment process within the first few visits and are usually willing and able to leverage their contact time by completing simple self-report forms.

The Clinical Monitoring Form (CMF) and the waiting room Self-Monitoring Form provided in Appendices 1 and 4 are standardized record keeping forms designed for clinicians to use as routine progress notes. The CMF records all the data required to determine the clinical status and over one hundred other clinically important variables. Using the patient self-report forms as a starting point, clinicians can usually elicit the information needed for a comprehensive progress note such as the CMF within 10 minutes. An additional 5–15 minutes is usually sufficient to complete a satisfactory collaborative treatment plan process. Very ill patients or patients unwilling to collaborate require additional time, but even so systematic assessment increases efficiency.

Use Graphical Charting To Identify Patterns

Knowledge of an individual patient's pattern of illness is perhaps the most useful guide to planning treatment, and is especially helpful if episodes are similar with regards to their prodrome, phase sequence, duration, or season of onset. The use of a graphical mood chart greatly enhances the psychiatrist's ability to recognize patterns of illness and the impact of each treatment. With modest encouragement from the clinician, patients can quickly learn to chart their mood, sleep pattern, and treatments on a daily basis (*see* Appendix 2). At follow-up, the mood chart can be reviewed and the information incorporated into the patient's chart. Over time, the accumulated mood chart data facilitates tracking of response to treatment, typical precipitants, cycle frequency, pattern of illness, and duration of episodes.

Education

Establishing a true collaborative alliance requires informed collaborators. Few healthcare systems can provide the resources required to deliver the considerable amount of education needed to give patients and their supports the fund of knowledge, or even the vocabulary, sufficient to participate meaningfully as collaborators in their own care. STEP-BD deals with this problem by supplementing clinical communication with enduring materials such as the STEP-BD collaborative care workbook and videotape (additional resources can be found in the Appendices). Such take-home materials enable patients to absorb information at times more favorable to learning and allow for the inclusion of significant others who may not be able to attend clinical visits.

Fundamentals of Disease Management: Iterative Measurement/Management

Accurate diagnostic assessment of the current mood state is crucial in choosing an effective intervention. It is often necessary to use non-mood stabilizing unimodal therapies, antidepressants, or neuroleptics, for acute and continuation phase treatment of depression and mania. Particular caution should be taken before ruling out the diagnosis of manic or mixed episode. Prescription of antidepressants to patients misdiagnosed as suffering from depression, who are actually suffering from a manic or mixed episode, may worsen an already serious clinical condition.

General Principles for Selection of Treatment Strategies

Three principles derived (listed below) from the Expert Consensus Guidelines can be applied to construct a "menu of reasonable choices" at each of the critical decision points.

1. Use proven treatments first.

2. Use a mood stabilizer in every phase of the illness.

3. Use a multiphase treatment strategy that targets the treatment plan to specific objectives as patients progress through phases of acute, continuation and maintenance treatment.

Note: Expert guidelines support the use of "mood stabilizers" for bipolar patients, but this widely-used term has no consensus scientific definition. For most clinicians this term is understood as a shorthand reference to lithium, carbamazepine, and valproate. As new medications enter the therapeutic market, there is a tendency to consider interventions with anticonvulsant or putative antimanic properties as "mood stabilizers" even in the absence of any data specific to their use in BD. Instead of perpetuating the use of this imprecise term, referring to medications in terms of their proven acute or prophylactic (anticycling) efficacy can improve the clarity of communication. The term "mood stabilizer" need not be expunged from our discourse, but should be limited and generally understood as a marketing rather than a medical term. In this spirit, use of the term "mood stabilizer" has been limited to instances where alternatives with less common usage might detract from the intended meaning.

Weighing Unequal Evidence

Using proven treatments first requires knowledge of the state of ever-changing literature and some critical evaluation of the available evidence. It is worth noting that, for many decisions, pertinent high-quality evidence might be totally lacking. Nevertheless, a good clinical manager will want to offer treatments based on the best available evidence and will want to assign weight to such forms of evidence as might be available. A simple grading system like the one frequently employed in the construction of evidence-based guidelines can also be utilized to inform the critical analysis needed to rank treatments.

The best quality of evidence comes from randomized, double-blind, placebo-controlled trials. This level of evidence merits an "A" rating when the trial has included an appropriate sample, sufficiently large to have at least an 80% chance of detecting a difference (statistical power) and provide confidence that the results are not due to chance alone. A detailed review of statistical considerations is beyond the scope of this book, but two points should be noted here. First, generally accepted statistical conventions allow the interpretation of results as significantly different when the probability that the observed difference is attributable to chance alone is 5% or less. Second, studies reporting differences insufficient to meet this standard merely fail to allow rejection of the null hypothesis and do not indicate that the conditions are the same. In other words, failure to detect a statistically significant difference does not mean that treatment conditions are equivalent.

For purposes of weighing evidence, an A+ might be reserved for those instances where less than 40 studies have been reported and more than one double-blind placebo-controlled study supports the same finding. An A- would indicate positive outcomes on some but not all relevant measures. Double-blind controlled trials without placebo or not completely satisfying the requirements above, would be graded "B". Open trials can be very valuable when controlled and are most informative when the treatments being compared are assigned by randomization. Such trials will be graded "C" and "C+", respectively. Uncontrolled observations are frequently problematic but case series and even single case reports can provide a rationale for selecting treatment and can be graded "D" and "D-", respectively. In the absence of published studies, treatments could be rated "E+" or "E-" depending on whether or not clear category A evidence supported a class effect treatment.

This rough guide to ranking treatments can help establish the evidence basis for grouping medications in the roughly equivalent ranks referred to below as "equipoise options" and used to create a menu of reasonable choices for patients. Note: The lack of high quality head-to-head comparison studies makes it difficult to justify ranking treatments within a grouping (eg, treatments with category A evidence). Quality of evidence for widely-used psychotropics is presented in Table 1.2.

Presenting Evidence-Based Management Options: Offer a Menu of Reasonable Choices

At each decision point, clinicians can offer patients an opportunity to collaborate in treatment planning by offering a choice among options they consider reasonable.

Quality of Evidence for Widely-Used Psychotropics				
	Prophylaxis ("Mood Stabilizer")	Acute Mania/Mixed	Acute Bipolar Depression	Rapid Cycling
Lithium	A+	A+	B	C-
Divalproex	A-	A+	D	D
Carbamazepine	D	A+	D	D
Lamotrigine	A+	F	A	A
Gabapentin	E-	F	D	D
Topiramate	E-	D	D	D
Oxcarbazepine	E-	D	E-	D
Aripiprazole	E-	A+	D	D
Clozapine	D	D	E	D
Haloperidol	D	A	E-	E-
Olanzapine	A	A+	A	D
Risperidone	E+	A+	D	D
Quetiapine	E+	A+	A	D
Ziprasidone	E+	A+	E-	E-
Omega 3	D	E-	F	F
Category A: Double-blind placebo-controlled trials with adequate samples				
Category B: Double-blind comparator studies with adequate samples				
Category C: Open trials with adequate samples				
Category D: Uncontrolled observation or controlled study with ambiguous result				
Category E: No published evidence, +/- clear evidence of a class effect				
Category F: Available evidence negative				

Table 1.2

An iterative collaborative process can be started by giving highest priority to patient preference in the selection of a treatment from the group of equipoise options. At the next decision point, the menu of reasonable choices for that patient will be modified by the outcome of the prior intervention. The feedback of measurement upon management is extremely valuable as it increases the chances for positive outcome. Patients should be reminded that extending the collaboration beyond selection of treatment to the disciplined keeping of records is key to maximizing the benefit of this iterative process.

Negotiate: Treatments not Taken Have no Chance to Work

Maintaining the positive therapeutic alliance by using a collaborative care model.

The variability of presentation, course of illness, and response to specific treatments require an iterative approach to treatment (*see* Table 1.3). Until more specific treatments

Bipolar Disorder and the Challenges Inherent to the Therapeutic Alliance
1. Chronic irregular course
2. Risks and benefits are borne by patient and family, but managed by doctor
3. Self-reports subject to perceptual distortion
4. The need to make provision for a readily available surrogate to whom the patient can entrust executive functions, when impaired by illness

Table 1.3

become available, reducing the number of trials and errors necessary to find beneficial treatments for individual patients relies on a rational systematic approach to treatment and assessment. The system of treatment offered below is not the only, or necessarily the best, one but represents one such systematic approach.

Weighing the relative risks and benefits of treatment decisions is a burden best shared. Nearly all treatment is voluntary; ultimately, patients decide what advice to take, and the easiest advice for anyone to accept is their own. Patients who understand the concept of self-interest in taking a therapy are more likely to adhere to it. Therefore, negotiation to reach agreement on a course of action is usually more productive than persuasion to accept what is presented simply on recommendation.

Over the course of bipolar illness there are unquestionably times when negotiation is impossible or inappropriate, but even then it is usually more helpful to review a patient's interests than simply to give persuasive recommendations. During well periods, appeals to informed self-interest are less prone to rejection than simply endorsing prophylactic treatment. Saying, for instance, "we agree about your diagnosis and you have had at least one episode during each of the last four years, so I must tell you that it's quite likely that you will have another episode in the coming year. Do you want to discuss options that might decrease the likelihood of a recurrence this year?", is usually more productive than saying, "You have bipolar disorder. Therefore, I want you to take medication that may prevent future episodes".

Consider Creative Options

Exploration of patients' needs and fears often leads to productive solutions. For instance, patients and families often disagree about when to start antimanic medication.

Patients may acknowledge the validity of family concerns about maintaining control in the face of an impending episode, but refuse antimanic medication out of fears related to sedation or long-term weight gain. Creative solutions might involve initiating treatment with a very low initial dose, starting over a holiday weekend or agreement to discontinue if weight gain exceeds 2 kg. Options like these allow the patient a measure of control and protection, which enables them to benefit from a therapeutic trial that might otherwise be unacceptable.

Avoid Unnecessary and Unrealistic Long-Term Commitments

There is no need for a patient to agree in advance to take a treatment for the rest of their life – treatments without benefit will be discontinued. Patients can always decide if the actual benefit they derive is worth the costs and adverse effects they experience. The clinician and patient should agree about the management plan on a trial basis and agree how the results will be measured. An iterative collaborative process requires a working relationship in which the reasonable choice most attractive to patient preference is given an opportunity to succeed or fail.

Aim for Concordance

Concordance is a concept distinct from compliance and adherence. Adherence is concerned with whether the prescribed treatment is taken. Concordance is the extent to which patients and care providers agree about which treatment is most appropriate. Fortunately, many patients do succeed while following plans that are unappealing to the clinician; continuing with whatever works is not a problem. The more therapeutic outcomes are unsatisfactory, the more full concordance becomes an important therapeutic objective. In the face of discordance, adherence is improbable. On the other hand, when non-adherence in the context of concordance is identified, therapeutic effort can shift from educating the patient about self-interest to building specific external supports to increase adherence (*see* Table 1.4).

Data collected at the Massachusetts General Hospital bipolar clinic suggest that it is relatively easy to achieve concordance regarding the need to treat acute episodes, especially depression. Following resolution of acute symptoms, however, concordance regarding the need to continue treatment preventively is far more difficult to attain. Patients who have rejected evidence-based treatment recommendations in favor of "self control" or "natural remedies" can, however, be influenced by documentation of poor outcomes. Discordance around treatment recommendations for substance abuse, psychosocial interventions, and lifestyle issues can undermine an otherwise beneficial treatment plan.

Eliminate Cycle-Promoting Agents

Medications which promote cycling, such as recreational psychotropics and any steroid medications, should be eliminated from the treatment regimen whenever

Management Priority Based on Concordance and Adherence		
	Patient and clinician view of most appropriate treatment plan	
	Concordant	Discordant
Adherent with treatment plan	Maintain concordance by recognition of collaborative therapeutic outcomes	Improve concordance by recognition of self-interest and options for improved therapeutic outcomes
Non-adherent with treatment plan	Build external supports	Establish therapeutic alliance Clarify areas of agreement Recognize outcomes in the absence of collaboration

Table 1.4

possible. The role of standard antidepressants remains controversial. Eliminating antidepressants from the treatment regimen appears to be the single most successful intervention for ending rapid cycling [6,7]. The author's clinical experience also suggests that discontinuation of antidepressants often has salutary effects on the cycle rate of non-rapid cycling bipolar illness. For bipolar patients who have remained stable for periods longer than one year, however, there are no data suggesting a need to alter chronic antidepressant use. Neuroleptics, particularly phenothiazines, have also been associated with rapid cycling, and some patients improve when these agents are discontinued. Evidence from clinical trials to date has not associated any atypical antipsychotic with an increased rate of post-mania depression or cycle acceleration. Reduction of stimulants (including caffeine) and bronchodilators (albuterol, theophylline, etc.) also appears beneficial.

Encourage Good Mood Hygiene

Treatment outcome can be improved in many cases by educating the patient and his or her family about the nature of the illness and principles of good mood hygiene. Participation in psychoeducational programs has been shown to significantly reduce relapse rates [8–10]. Although studies associating environmental events with onset of episodes find little correlation beyond the earliest episodes, most patients are able to learn simple strategies to lessen conflict or avoid precipitants. Advising patients about the need to maintain stable sleep/wake, diet, and exercise schedules, the need to avoid extremes in work, and the need to take care when traveling across time zones is often beneficial. Mood hygiene can be improved by helping family members deal constructively with the hostility aroused in relating to the bipolar patient [11]. The impact of negative expressed emotion seems particularly strong in the early phase of an episode and during the period immediately following discharge from the hospital. Teaching families to limit negative expressed emotion may be facilitated by

13

disciplined use of a constructive disengagement strategy in the face of provocation or building hostility.

Although, like many of the somatic therapies described below, there are no empirical data showing the effectiveness of good mood hygiene in treatment-refractory bipolar patients, the low cost and low risk associated with these strategies justifies their recommendation.

Encourage Participation in Psychosocial Treatment

Since bipolar illness tends to be understood in biological terms, it is interesting that psychotherapy appears beneficial for bipolar patients. Verbal therapies do not claim acute antimanic benefits, but most forms of psychotherapy seem to augment the prophylactic benefit of lithium [12–20]. While the active elements of psychotherapy remain unclear, the prophylactic efficacy of verbal therapies, as with lithium treatment, appear to require continued treatment.

The impact of expressed emotion may also play a role in psychotherapy. Numerous anecdotes suggest that during episodes of mania or severe depression, insight-oriented therapies can have destabilizing effects on mood state. Recently, data has appeared suggesting that bipolar patients with more severe illness may actually worsen in response to psychosocial interventions. Therapists treating bipolar patients can improve mood hygiene by assessing mood state and making appropriate adjustments to the content, frequency, and duration of therapy sessions. As patients become acutely ill, it is most appropriate for sessions to become more frequent but briefer, with a focus on safety issues and control of acute symptoms. Many patients report beneficial experiences from self-help groups such as the Depression and Bipolar Support Alliance (DBSA) and the National Alliance for the Mentally Ill (NAMI).

Using a Multiphase Treatment Strategy to Link Management to Assessment of Current Clinical Status

The clinician should implement a specific treatment plan based on the current therapeutic priority of individual patients (*see* Table 1.5); determination of clinical priority is of the utmost importance. The wide range of potentially appropriate treatments might be sequenced and dosed very differently for individuals at the same decision point. The collaborative care model begins by determining – based on the patient's current diagnosis, symptom profile, and past history – whether priority should be given to tolerability or efficacy, and organizing treatment tactics around the strategy which best serves the current priority.

- The sequential care strategy gives the highest priority to tolerability.

- The urgent care strategy gives highest priority to immediate efficacy.

Multiphase Treatment Strategy
Sequential versus urgent care
Prioritize in accordance with acute-, continuation-, and maintenance-phase objectives
Menu of reasonable choices to provide equipoise options = Evidence (efficacy/individual)
Offer an optimal trial for assessment of benefit:burden

Table 1.5

As with other medical conditions, such as hypertension, risk assessment drives the treatment priorities. A mildly hypertensive patient might be offered diet and exercise, and should that prove ineffective, a diuretic and then a beta blocker. In this sequential care scenario, the most benign untried option available is offered at each decision point. An urgent care approach might be offered to patients suffering from malignant hypertension. Urgent care options might sacrifice tolerability for the potential life-saving benefit of intravenous antihypertensive treatment.

The general approach outlined above enables the psychiatrist to choose the appropriate specific strategy for a patient's circumstances. The strategy selected provides the organizing principle for assembling the reasonable treatments in the most desirable sequence for individual patients (within each treatment pathway). Treatment trials are carried out until clinical objectives are met, the trial is declared ineffective (due to lack of response at maximal tolerated dose), or adverse effects force a change in treatment. The treatment guidelines presented below illustrate this procedure.

Several dimensions are involved in the progression of steps in these guidelines. Each set of guidelines presents a sequence of treatment categories and each category lists a sequence of individual agents. Phase of treatment is an important dimension of treatment strategy over time, because treatment adjustments are required in order to achieve the different goals and address the different problems of each phase. (Simple guidelines for acute mania, mixed episodes, bipolar depression, rapid cycling, and maintenance treatment are presented in subsequent chapters.)

Phase of Treatment

The treatment phases defined by Kupfer [21] for unipolar illness can also be applied to bipolar illness. The complex task of treatment planning can be streamlined by considering the changing needs of patients specific to the acute, continuation, and maintenance phases (*see* Figure 1.3).

15

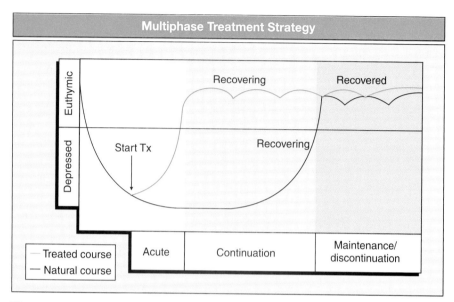

Figure 1.3. Tx, treatment.

Acute phase

The acute phase begins when the patient meets the criteria for an episode (depression, mania, hypomania, or mixed) and treatment is initiated. Each individual trial of acute treatment is carried out to one of three endpoints:

1) discontinuation because the patient is unable to tolerate the adverse effects of treatment;

2) discontinuation because the patient has failed to respond to a maximal trial of the treatment (including, if warranted, augmentation strategies); or

3) treatment has resolved the acute episode.

Problems that may arise during the acute phase include treatment intolerance, inadequate dosage, partial response, and non-response. Treatments are adjusted or replaced as necessary to manage these problems until the acute symptoms remit, thus ending the acute phase.

Avoid exotic polypharmacy! The acute phase also offers an important opportunity to replace any treatments that may have failed to prevent the current episode, as well as any treatment initiated during this phase and considered ineffective.

16

Continuation Phase

A clinical status of "recovering" indicates remission of acute symptoms and defines the continuation phase of treatment. Relapse with return of full syndromal or continued symptomatic status is the most frequently encountered problem during the continuation phase. Successful acute therapies are, therefore, continued at full dosage for a period of time to prevent relapse. With the remission of symptoms, the continuation phase is also a time when denial of illness fosters noncompliance. A decision to return to work or school in the first weeks of the continuation phase often proves premature. Brief periods of well-being do not guarantee the end of an episode.

The length of the continuation phase is based on the clinician's estimate of the period necessary to exceed the likely (natural) duration of the episode in the absence of treatment. Whether the estimated duration of the continuation phase is determined on the basis of the patient's prior episodes or based on a more general estimate of the likely duration of depressive or manic episodes, the purpose of the continuation phase is to avoid relapse. This is most often accomplished by maintaining treatment at the levels required to induce remission, but may involve titration of the dosage. Some treatment-responsive patients may benefit by dose reduction during the continuation phase if the side effects of medication substantially negate the gains due to remission of mood symptoms. A larger group will intermittently experience significant symptoms during the continuation phase (continued symptomatic) which, while not fulfilling the criteria for an acute depressive episode, may warrant an increase in antidepressant (or antimanic) treatments.

The continuation phase ends and the discontinuation phase or maintenance phase begins when the patient is declared to have recovered from the acute episode.

Discontinuation Phase/Maintenance Phase

The discontinuation phase follows a decision to discontinue a treatment and involves monitoring for recurrence while gradually tapering medication. This process may result in some medications intended for acute-phase use becoming a part of the maintenance regimen. If, for instance, gradual discontinuation of antimanic or antidepressant medication used for acute phase treatment proved to be destabilizing, this individual experience could justify recommending the medication as part of the maintenance phase treatment plan.

A decision to redirect the therapeutic focus away from treatment of the preceding acute episode toward maintaining recovery or preventing the recurrence of future acute episodes launches the maintenance phase.

Optimize Mood Stabilizing Therapies

After controlling the symptoms in the acute phase, the next treatment priority is preventing recurrence (*see* Figure 1.4). Using an iterative approach, mood stabilizing

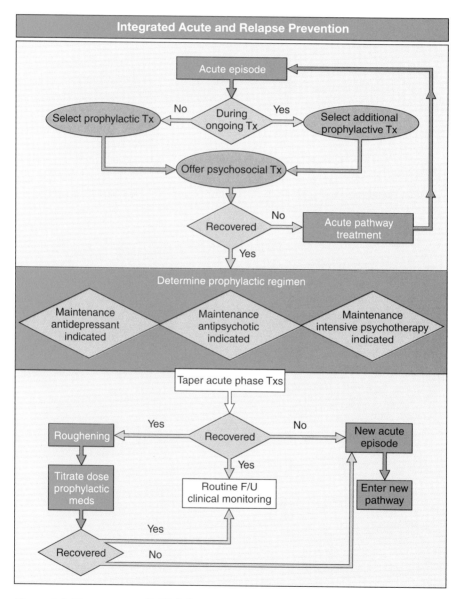

Figure 1.4. Tx, treatment; F/U, follow-up.

therapies are presented in a step-wise fashion, and the impact of each treatment on cycle length is assessed based on follow-up assessment and mood charting. A period equivalent to three times the patient's cycle length and not less than six months is usually required for confident determination of prophylactic benefit [22]. Partially effective or ineffective therapies can be discontinued or augmented by adjunctive mood stabilizing agents.

Monitor for Roughening

Many patients experience intermittent subsyndromal symptoms (roughening) during the discontinuation/maintenance phase. The significance of roughening depends on whether it is the harbinger of an impending acute episode or is merely a brief period of mild symptoms with little clear relation to the patient's mood disorder. Studies of such interepisode symptoms done by Keller [23] and Fava [24] suggest that roughening with features of depression often resolves without intervention. Symptoms of hypomania carry a higher risk of evolving into full affective episodes. The occurrence of roughening can be managed by increasing the dose of prophylactic treatments and shortening the follow-up interval. The occurrence of symptoms meeting criteria for an acute episode would be considered a recurrence (new episode) requiring reintroduction of acute treatments.

How long should maintenance therapy continue? There is considerable debate as to when lifetime prophylaxis should be recommended. This complex debate need not impede most routine treatment since in many important areas there is broad consensus among experts. Expert consensus supports at least one year of prophylaxis following the first manic episode and any subsequent manic episode. There is also general agreement that patients with three or more episodes warrant long-term maintenance therapy.

Selection of Specific Agents

At present no symptom or laboratory profiles have been found which allow selection of medication on the basis of predicted markers of response. In the absence of these predictors, drugs can be selected on the basis of known personal or family history of response, the need to treat comorbid conditions, matching adverse-effect profiles to ameliorate acute target symptoms, or strong patient preference.

Even in cases where other selection factors are likely determinants of treatment selection (eg, patient's mother responded to doxepin), it is useful to discuss risks and adverse-effect profiles in the context of the other choices the treating psychiatrist might deem reasonable for an individual patient. Better informed patients who know what to expect from medications they have been involved in choosing are likely to find it easier to maintain fidelity to their treatment plan.

The practical tables provided elsewhere in this book are intended to be used as an aide in discussing with patients which medications the clinician regards as the most reasonable choices for an individual. Generally, it is useful to review the information in the practical table, encourage the patient to participate in selecting from among the reasonable choices, and provide the patient with a copy of the relevant table.

Managing a Treatment Trial

Initiate treatment in a manner that anticipates potential problems. Take particular care to avoid problems that might lead a patient to prematurely discard a treatment they had selected as the most desirable. Patient and family education is the best means of avoiding this early stumbling block. The collaborative approach recommends reviewing the practical tables with the patient and available supports, with emphasis on the intended initial dosage, time of administration, possible side effects, and which adverse experiences should trigger additional contact with the clinician.

Where multiple forms of the same medication are available it is more desirable to begin by offering treatment with the form likely to be best tolerated rather than switching to the better tolerated form after adverse effects occur. Split dosing can also be employed as required to enhance tolerability, but compliance drops with multiple daily dosing. Once daily is usually the most desirable dosing schedule, if tolerated. Similarly for elderly patients and those with greater sensitivity to particular adverse effects, initial doses may need to be lowered from those recommended in the practical tables (*see* chapter 8).

Indications for Nonstandard Treatments: Unproven Exploratory Options

In any of the variety of circumstances in which use of nonstandard or innovative treatments (*see* Table 1.6) may be appropriate, care should be taken to document the indication in the medical record and to ensure that the patient is aware when nonstandard treatment is administered. The indication for nonstandard treatment initiated by the clinician is strongest for patients who have severe episodes refractory to multiple standard treatments. Adjunctive use of innovative treatments known to be compatible with standard treatments is also generally preferred prior to use of treatments of unknown safety and unproven efficacy.

Indications for Nonstandard Treatment	
Indication	**Example**
Standard treatments have failed	Use of stimulant after nonresponse to >1 standard antidepressants
Standard treatments are intolerable	Use of DHEA in patient with a history of severe headache during prior treatment with multiple standard agents with different mechanisms/structure
Innovative treatment compatible with standard treatment	Patient requests adjunctive use of omega-3 fatty acids
Standard treatments are unacceptable	Patient refuses standard treatments because of fears based on knowledge of individuals with unfavorable outcome

Table 1.6. DHEA, dehydroepiandrosterone.

References

1. Lopez AD, Murray CC. **The global burden of disease, 1990–2020.** *Nat Med* 1998; **4**:1241–1243.

2. Angst F, Stassen HH, Clayton PJ *et al.* **Mortality of patients with mood disorders: follow-up over 34–38 years.** *J Affect Disord* 2002; **68**:167–181.

3. Harvard Bipolar Research Program. www.manicdepressive.org (last accessed December 2003).

4. Fava GA. **Subclinical symptoms in mood disorders: pathophysiological and therapeutic implications.** *Psychol Med* 1999; **29**:47–61.

5. Keller MB, Lavori PW, Kane JM *et al.* **Subsyndromal symptoms in bipolar disorder. A comparison of standard and low serum levels of lithium.** *Arch Gen Psychiatry* 1992; **49**:371–376.

6. Wehr TA, Sack DA, Rosenthal NE *et al.* **Rapid cycling affective disorder: contributing factors and treatment responses in 51 patients.** *Am J Psychiatry* 1988; **145**:179–184.

7. Kukopulos AD, Reginaldi D, Laddomada P *et al.* **Course of the manic-depressive cycle and changes caused by treatment.** *Pharmakopsychiatr Neuropsychopharmakol* 1980; **13**:156–167.

8. Reinares M, Colom F, Martinez-Aran A *et al.* **Therapeutic interventions focused on the family of bipolar patients.** *Psychother Psychosom* 2002; **71**:2–10.

9. Colom F, Vieta E, Martinez-Aran A *et al.* **A randomized trial on the efficacy of group psychoeducation in the prophylaxis of recurrences in bipolar patients whose disease is in remission.** *Arch Gen Psychiatry* 2003; **60**:402–407.

10. Rea MM, Tompson MC, Miklowitz DJ *et al.* **Family-focused treatment versus individual treatment for bipolar disorder: results of a randomized clinical trial.** *J Consult Clin Psychol* 2003; **71**:482–492.

11. Priebe S, Wildgrube C, Muller-Oerlinghausen B *et al.* **Lithium prophylaxis and expressed emotion.** *Br J Psychiatry* 1989; **154**:396–399.

12. Mayo JA. **Marital therapy with manic-depressive patients treated with lithium.** *Compr Psychiatry* 1979; **20**:419–426.

13. Lesser IM, Godofsky ID. **Group treatment for chronic patients: educational and supervisory aspects.** *Int J Group Psychother* 1983; **33**:535–546.

14. Vasile RG, Samson JA, Bemporad J *et al.* **A biopsychosocial approach to treating patients with affective disorders.** *Am J Psychiatry* 1987; **144**:341–344.

15. Miklowitz DJ, Goldstein MJ, Nuechterlein KH *et al.* **Family factors and the course of bipolar affective disorder.** *Arch Gen Psychiatry* 1988; **45**:225–231.

16. Van Gent EM, Via SL, Zwart FM. **Group therapy in addition to lithium therapy in patients with bipolar disorder.** *Acta Psychiatr Belg* 1988; **88**:405–418.

17. Kanas N. **Group psychotherapy with bipolar patients: a review and synthesis.** *Int J Group Psychother* 1993; **43**:321–333.

18. Miklowitz DJ , Richards JA, Geirge EL *et al.* **Integrated family and individual therapy for bipolar disorder: results of a treatment development study.** *J Clin Psychiatry* 2003; **64**:182–191.

19. Miklowitz DJ, George EL, Richards JA *et al.* **A randomized study of family-focused psychoeducation and pharmacotherapy in the outpatient management of bipolar disorder.** *Arch Gen Psychiatry* 2003; **60**:904–912.

20. Lam DH, Watkins ER, Hayward P *et al.* **A randomized controlled study of cognitive therapy for relapse prevention for bipolar affective disorder: outcome of the first year.** *Arch Gen Psychiatry* 2003; **60**:145–152.

21. Kupfer DJ. **Maintenance treatment in recurrent depression: current and future directions. The first William Sargant Lecture.** *Br J Psychiatry* 1992; **161**:309–316.

22. Post RM, Kramlinger KG, Altshuler LL *et al.* **Treatment of rapid cycling bipolar illness.** *Psychopharmacol Bull* 1990; **26**:37–47.

23. Keller MB, Lavori PW, Kane JM *et al.* **Subsyndromal symptoms in bipolar disorder. A comparison of standard and low serum levels of lithium.** *Arch Gen Psychiatry* 1992; **49**:371–376.

24. Fava GA, Kellner R. **Prodromal symptoms in affective disorders.** *Am J Psychiatry* 1991; **48**:823–830.

Chapter 2

Basics of Bipolar Disorder

Bipolar disorders (BDs) are chronic multidimensional conditions characterized by an irregular course of acute episodes, a high frequency of subsyndromal interepisode symptomatology, and comorbid conditions. Along with the episodes which define mood disorders, the nonaffective psychopathology (eg, anxiety, cognitive impairment) and general medical conditions (eg, obesity, migraine headache) frequently associated with BD should be understood as the expression of an as yet poorly understood underlying pathophysiology. It seems likely that several mechanisms might produce common phenotypes and that environmental factors modify genotypic expression. Understanding these mechanisms would greatly aid diagnosis and help direct treatment, but currently clinicians must manage patients while largely ignorant of these relationships.

The complexity of symptomatology often leads to confusion, which adds frustration and undermines confidence in treatment decisions. The basic fund of knowledge related to BD and its nosology presented below is intended to facilitate the processes of clinical diagnosis and management over the course of bipolar illness. After discussion of these issues, a simple process of systematizing evaluation of information gathered during clinical assessment (beyond the evaluation of current clinical status) is offered, the aim being to improve diagnostic confidence.

Understanding DSM-IV Mood Disorder Nosology

Emil Kraepelin, the father of the modern mood disorder concept, recognized the inherent unreliability of basing the system of psychiatric diagnosis on signs and symptoms. Kraepelin coined the term manic-depressive insanity for the condition he differentiated from dementia and schizophrenia on the basis of longitudinal factors; early age of onset, and course of illness (rather than on cross-sectional symptoms) [1]. He found that manic-depressive illness had peak onset during late adolescence and early adulthood, and that the periods of illness were characterized by prominent mood symptoms. He regarded the differences between predominant mood states – euphoria, irritability, and depression – as slight in comparison to the similarity in the course marked by well periods with full restitution of function. Leonhard [2,3] attempted to classify psychiatric illness into two large groups based on whether symptoms were consistently of one type or fluctuated between opposite presentations. Only one of the 13 bipolar type illnesses he proposed was validated, the monopolar and bipolar mood disorders. Three independent family studies presented in 1966 by Angst, Perris, and

Winokur found more bipolar relatives in the families of bipolar probands than in the families of unipolar probands, which led to the modern division of mood disorders into unipolar and bipolar [4,5].

The third edition of the Diagnostic and Statistical Manual (DSM-III) introduced operational criteria for diagnosis of mania and depression, and used the occurrence of a manic episode as the defining characteristic of BD. In the fourth edition of the manual (DSM-IV), nosology for mood disorders provides criteria for classification at three conceptual levels [6]. At the conceptual level of lifetime mood disorder diagnoses, the criteria for the separate primary mood disorders (unipolar mood disorder, bipolar mood disorder, and their subtypes) are based largely on the history of diagnosed episodes. Thus, the criteria defining discrete abnormal mood states – which DSM-IV designates as depression, hypomania, mania, or mixed episodes (*see* Table 2.1 for a modified summary) – are the building blocks underlying diagnosis of lifetime disorder and subtype. The occurrence of even a single period of abnormal mood elevation not attributable to substance abuse or a general medical condition is the cardinal feature of BDs. The occurrence of major depressive episodes (MDE) and hypomanias comprises the bipolar II diagnosis. If a patient previously diagnosed with bipolar II suffers an episode meeting the full criteria for mania, the lifetime diagnosis would be changed to bipolar I. The DSM does not include age of onset or course of illness as diagnostic criteria for mood disorders.

Course specifiers, a third conceptual dimension, do not represent separate pathological conditions, but merely lay out criteria defining common patterns in the course of episodes with the defined DSM-IV mood disorders rather than separate disorders. Rapid cycling requires the occurrence of four episodes or two complete cycles over a 12-month period. Postpartum onset refers to episodes within four weeks of delivery of a child. The seasonal pattern course specifier requires a temporal relationship between onset of episodes and time of year in the majority of episodes and that no episode has occurred outside the expect interval over the preceding two years.

DSM-IV Criteria for Episodes: the Building Blocks of Lifetime Diagnosis

The criteria for DSM-IV mood episodes all require a predominant mood state persisting over a defined period (of minimum duration) during which several associated features must be present at or above a threshold level of intensity. When substance abuse or a general medical condition is identified as the causative factor producing the mood syndrome, episodes are diagnosed using the same criteria but must be diagnosed as secondary depression, secondary mania etc.

Summary of DSM-IV Episodes			
Episode Type	Predominant Mood State	Duration and Symptom Threshold	Associated Features
Mania	High, happy, euphoric, expansive, irritable	At least 1 week With ≥3 symptoms present to a significant degree or any duration if hospitalized	1. Increased self-esteem/grandiosity 2. Decreased need for sleep 3. More talkative 4. Racing thought/flight of ideas 5. Distractible 6. Increase goal directed activities/ psychomotor agitation 7. Risk taking (potential painful consequences)
Hypomania	High, happy, euphoric, expansive, irritable	At least 4 days With ≥3 symptoms present to a significant degree	1. Increased self-esteem/grandiosity 2. Decreased need for sleep 3. More talkative 4. Racing thoughts/flight of ideas 5. Distractible 6. Increased goal directed activities/ psychomotor agitation 7. Risk taking (potential painful consequences)
Depression	Low, sad, disinterested	At least 2 weeks With ≥5 symptoms most of the day/nearly every day	1. Sleep disturbance 2. Diminished interest 3. Guilt/low self-esteem 4. Decreased energy 5. Inability to concentrate/make simple decisions 6. Appetite disturbance 7. Psychomotor retardation/ agitation 8. Suicidal ideation/morbid preoccupation
Mixed	Both high and low states above	At least 1 week With symptoms most of the day/nearly every day	Associated features present which fulfil both mania and depression

Table 2.1

What is Mania?

Mania, often depicted in somewhat positive terms, (eg, abundant energy, productivity, and feeling great) is a serious medial condition that usually presents with considerable dysphoria and most often requires hospital admission. Field tests find DSM-IV diagnostic criteria for mania highly reliable. The key to reliability is not the presence of any one symptom, but rather the constellation of

25

symptoms within the defined seven-day time frame. During this time of elevated mood, several associated symptoms – that go beyond the bounds of experience in the general population or the individual's usual behavioral characteristics – must be present to a significant degree.

DSM-IV requires the persistence of an abnormally expansive, euphoric, or irritable mood state and at least three associated features of mania to a marked degree over at least seven days, unless the patient is hospitalized. In the absence of expansive or euphoric mood, irritable mood and four associated symptoms are required, plus significant impairment in social or occupation function. The impairment is often evident due to the consequences of risk taking, but the DSM criteria require only that behavior has potentially painful consequences. These criteria can be met by engaging in risky activities without necessarily getting caught or experience of actual consequences.

Patients, however, tend to experience moods as more transient and may be insensitive to their degree of impairment during manic states. Collateral informants can be very helpful, but cannot eliminate the difficulties of distinguishing abnormal mood states from common emotional experience. A smile, laugh, or very brief upturn in a patient's sense of well-being does not constitute mania, unless it is part of a recurrent inappropriate behavioral syndrome. Extreme mood states lasting more than two hours are unusual in the general population, but brief elevated mood states must be recurrent through the course of seven days if they are to satisfy the DSM-IV criteria.

What is Hypomania?

The term "hypomania" refers to a clearly abnormal mood state with mild to severe symptoms of mania that may last for a few days or may persist for many months.

The key difference between mania and hypomania is not symptoms *per se* but the extent of functional impairment. Mania can cause enormous problems in daily functioning, and often leads to serious problems with a person's relationships or work activities. By definition, hypomania does not cause problems to the same extent as mania, and for some patients, hypomania can be a pleasant state of good humor and high productivity. Unfortunately, for most people even hypomanic symptoms of durations shorter than four days can be problematic. Things said and done during a hypomanic episode often have negative long-term consequences. For example, during a hypomanic episode, buying more clothes than necessary might delay rent payments, or telling off-color jokes may bring positive attention at the office party but might ultimately lessen chances for promotion. Hypomania may occur as a prelude to a full manic episode or it may precede a severe depression. The diagnosis of hypomania is far less reliable than the diagnosis of mania or major depression.

What is Depression?

Depression is an unfortunate term because its indiscriminate usage leads to misunderstanding in communication with non-psychiatric medical personnel as well as with patients and their family members. Depression is a label commonly applied to non-clinical emotional states as well as being used to designate a range of dysphoric states (including states meeting DSM-IV criteria for MDE). Often patients suffering MDE differ from the general population more by their loss of the ability to experience pleasure in activities that they usually find fun or exciting, than the degree to which they feel sad.

The DSM-IV criteria for MDE require the presence of five symptoms most of the day nearly every day for two weeks or longer and must include depressed mood or decreased interest.

It is not uncommon for people who are depressed to feel helpless and hopeless about treatment as well as about their life situation. It is usually more helpful to acknowledge the patient's suffering than to attempt to persuade them that their view is distorted. Maintaining your therapeutic optimism is important. Most patients are willing to accept treatment you present as potentially beneficial, even when their illness tells them there is no possibility of getting better. The benefits of a therapeutic alliance can be lost by over-promising the potential rate or extent to which treatment will relieve symptoms.

What are Mixed Episodes?

The DSM-IV criteria for a mixed episode require occurrence of an episode with enough associated features to meet the full criteria for mania and depression over a one-week period. Episodes meeting these stringent criteria are notoriously difficult to treat. Research reporting encouraging results for similar sounding conditions (eg, mixed mania, dysphoria mania, depressive mania) often require full episodes of mania for enrollment, but include subjects with subsyndromal as well as full depressive episodes. As few as two depressive symptoms predict relative nonresponse to lithium, but no treatment has been proven efficacious for episodes meeting the full DSM-IV syndromal criteria.

Subtypes of Bipolar Disorder

The DSM-IV divides BD into four subtypes, which reflect the types of episodes that have occurred over an individual's lifetime (*see* Tables 2.2 and 2.3).

Summary of Unipolar and Bipolar Disorder Subtypes			
	Mania	Hypomania	Depression (MDE)
Unipolar disorders			
Major depression	No	No	Yes
Dysthymia disorder	No	No	1–2 years, without full MDE but chronically feels sad or down
Bipolar disorders			
Bipolar I	Yes	Yes	Usually, but not required
Bipolar II	No	Yes	Yes
Cyclothymia	No	Yes	1–2 years, without full MDE, but frequent high and unstable mood
Bipolar NOS	No	Yes	May experience MDE. Often some symptoms of depression
Or			
Bipolar NOS	No	Some symptoms of hypomania	Yes

Table 2.2. MDE, major depressive episode; NOS, not otherwise specified.

Summary of DSM-IV Course Specifiers	
Rapid cycling	4 or more episodes in a 1-year period
Postpartum onset	Onset of mania, hypomania, or depression within 4 weeks of childbirth
Seasonal pattern	Over several years, most episodes typically start (and end) at the same time each year

Table 2.3

The definition of bipolar I is based on the occurrence of a full manic episode; about 90% of bipolar I patients also suffer episodes of major depression, but these are not required for the diagnosis.

The designation bipolar II is given to patients who have never experienced a full manic episode, but have experienced at least one hypomanic episode and at least one episode of major depression.

Cyclothymia refers to forms of bipolar illness which include an index period of chronic mood instability (one year for children or adolescents, two years for adults). During the majority of the index period days, patients experience abnormal mood states, including frequent hypomanic symptoms, but never reach full criteria for either mania or major depression. Cyclothymia is not excluded when full episodes occur outside the required index diagnostic period of mood instability.

DSM-IV designates patients with periods of clearly abnormal mood elevation failing to meet criteria for any of these three defined subtypes (eg, hypomanias only) as bipolar, not otherwise specified (NOS). For example, a person can have some symptoms of hypomania followed by an episode of depression. Because the symptoms of hypomania were too brief or too few to meet the full criteria for hypomania, the person would not qualify as bipolar II, but they would qualify for a diagnosis of bipolar NOS (also sometime referred to as "atypical bipolar" disorder).

In summary, what distinguishes BDs from unipolar disorders is the occurrence of episodes of abnormally high, expansive, or irritable mood (eg, hypomania or mania). Episodes of depression (low mood) are a common feature of BD. Psychotic features are frequently associated with depression, mania, or mixed episodes and do not differentiate BD from schizophrenia. Roughly 50–75% of manic episodes and about 5–10% of depressive episodes include psychotic features (hallucination, delusions, formal thought disorder).

Schizoaffective Disorder

This is a separate category of major psychiatric illness. The DSM-IV criteria require at least one affective episode meeting full criteria for mania or depression and the presence of psychotic features (hallucinations or delusions) which persist for at least two weeks beyond the resolution of the mood episode. Schizoaffective patients who have experienced a mania have a prognosis between that of BD and schizophrenia.

Epidemiology and Course of Illness

Most epidemiological studies find the prevalence of bipolar I disorder is about 1% (range 0.5–1.2%) and a female:male gender ratio close to 1:1 [7]. With the inclusion of patients with periods of mood elevation milder than full manic episodes, the reported lifetime prevalence for all subtypes of bipolar illness ranges from 3–12% [8–10].

Typically, the first episode of BD has its onset during the second or third decade of life (peak age of onset 15–25 years). The initial episode may be followed by a longer remission than subsequent episodes (4.5 years median). Some studies have suggested that the periods of remission shrink progressively over the course of the first three to five episodes and then tend to stabilize, with an average of about one episode per year [11–13]. More recent data corrected for number of episodes also suggest an average of about one per year, but find a more constant rate of recurrence. These longitudinal studies do not support the kindling hypothesis, which predicts continuous acceleration of cycling over the lifecycle.

Over the first ten years, the average bipolar patient will have about four major mood episodes. For most individuals, over the long-term, episodes of mood elevation will be fewer and briefer than the depressed episodes, although some may have an equal number of depressive and manic episodes. During 15-years' follow-up, Judd found that the percentage of weeks that bipolar I and bipolar II subjects experienced depression was 31% and 52%, respectively. In contrast, hypomania, mania, and mixed episodes were reported during only 10% of weeks by bipolar I subjects, and bipolar II subjects reported 1.6% of weeks with hypomania [14]. Furthermore, patients experienced subsyndromal states (equivalent to the clinical status described in Chapter 1 as "continued symptomatic" or "roughening") three times more often than full syndromal states.

These data reveal two important realities related to the concept of discrete episodes over the course of BD. First, even among patients who have frequent severe episodes, there may be long periods with normal mood state. Some doctors, patients, and family members may be tempted to interpret prolonged periods of wellness as evidence that the diagnosis of BD was incorrect. Unfortunately, this is seldom the case. The natural course of BD often includes periods of remission, but without treatment, those who meet criteria for BD will almost always relapse. Second, episodes are often not as discrete nor recoveries as complete as those described in classic pre-DSM-III conceptualizations of manic depressive illness. It is an error to regard patients as well simply because their symptoms do not currently meet the criteria for diagnosis of depression or mania. In fact, much of the disability associated with BD stems from the continued serious impairment experienced during chronic subsyndromal states.

Bipolar illness is associated not only with decreased quality of life for patients and their families, but also with high utilization of psychiatric and general medical services [15], and increased mortality rates due to suicide and other medical conditions [16,17]. Lish *et al.* estimated that BD reduces life expectancy by ten years and costs the afflicted individual an average of nine years of productive adult life [18]. In a sample of bipolar I subjects, Kessler found that 48% have made at least one suicide attempt [19]. A history of suicide attempt was recorded for 35.7% of 1000 bipolar I and bipolar II subjects entering the Systematic Treatment Enhancement Program for Bipolar Disorder (STEP-BD) [20]. Adjusted mortality rates are higher for untreated patients but are higher still (by an order of magnitude) for untreated bipolar patients with comorbid alcohol or substance abuse [21,22] (*see* Figure 2.1).

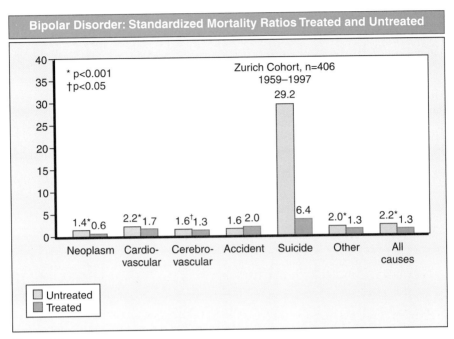

Figure 2.1

Psychiatric Comorbidities

The DSM-IV lists more than 330 different types of psychiatric disorders. It is uncommon to find a patient with BD who does not meet criteria for one or more additional DSM-IV disorders. Kessler found 100% of bipolar I patients meet criteria for at least one other axis I disorder [19]. The most frequent – anxiety disorders, alcohol and substance abuse, and attention deficit disorder – all appear to have substantial negative impact on the course of bipolar illness. The relationship between comorbid conditions and BD is likely to be bidirectional. Successful treatment of BD usually improves these conditions. Likewise, successful treatment of these conditions may improve the symptoms of BD. Unfortunately for some patients, the treatments for other disorders can worsen symptoms of BD. For example, antidepressant medicines used to treat obsessive-compulsive disorder and stimulants used to treat attention deficit disorder often worsen symptoms of BD and can even cause a manic episode.

Because of shared features such as impulsivity and dramatic mood instability, personality disorders (particularly borderline personality disorder) sometimes cause a diagnostic dilemma. The DSM-IV classification allows concurrent axis I and axis II diagnoses, but a desire for parsimony often leads clinicians to choose one or the other. Some cases defy classification, but disciplined attention in the diagnostic assessment to identification of a clear cut episode of mania, determination of age of onset, and deferring assignment of a personality pending reliable assessment of characteristic behaviors outside of affective episodes can usually add a substantial measure of clarity to the assessment.

What Causes Bipolar Disorder?

The cause of BD is unknown, and there are no useful biological markers or laboratory tests for the condition. BD does run in families, but does not have a simple Mendelian pattern of inheritance. Instead, it is presumed that many genes of small effect contribute to BD.

Environmental factors must also play a role in the development of bipolar illness since even identical twins are frequently discordant for BD [23–26].

Sleep deprivation and circadian rhythm disturbances have been implicated as a final common pathway leading to mania [27]. Hypothalamo-pituitary-adrenal axis abnormalities, thyroid abnormalities, neurotransmitter/receptor imbalances (especially involving dopaminergic activity), second messenger abnormalities, and mitochondrial dysfunction have all been associated with BD.

Recent neuroimaging and postmortem histopathology studies have focused interest on areas of the prefrontal cortex, amygdala, and hippocampus. Dysfunction in these areas may result from loss of glia and/or neurons, and reflect diminished nutrients or other factors essential for neuroprotection. The role of glia in regulating neuronal nutrition, nerve growth factors and excitatory amino acid neurotransmitter makes this an attractive hypothesis.

What are Risk versus Protective Factors in Coping with Bipolar Disorder?

A variety of factors may influence the risk of recurrence. Most of the putative protective strategies are intuitive rather than evidence-based: taking medications appropriately; using social, family, and community supports; using communication or problem-solving skills; utilizing treatment resources like psychotherapy; and avoiding risk factors. Strategies utilizing these protective factors while avoiding risk factors can be used to help patients develop a personalized collaborative care plan (*see* Table 2.4).

Protective and Risk Factors in Bipolar Disorder	
Protective Factors	**Risk Factors**
Use of prophylactic medications	Alcohol
Abstinence from alcohol	Recreational drug use
Abstinence from recreational drug use	Abrupt discontinuation of medications
Structured schedule	Antimanic agents
Regular awakening and sleep times	Antidepressants
Schedule of recurring social activity	Anxiolytics
Support system	Sleep disruption
Professionals	Loss of supports
Family	Cognitive distortions
Friends	Interpersonal conflict
Psychotherapy	Role transition
Good nutrition	Negative expressed emotion
	East–West travel
	Stress

Table 2.4

Problems in Diagnosis of Bipolar Disorder

Experienced clinicians and researchers debate whether BD is under-diagnosed or over-diagnosed, but there is no debating that it is often poorly diagnosed [18,28–30]. There are no diagnostic laboratory tests for BD and signs and symptoms are unreliable.

Lish *et al.* report that nearly a decade passes from onset of the first clear cut episode before bipolar patients are correctly diagnosed [18]. The long timelag between onset of illness and diagnosis leaves patients exposed not only to the stigma and impairment of their illness, but also to the potential mistreatment that can accompany misdiagnosis, the possibility that their illness will progress to a less treatable stage before they receive treatment, and to the excess mortality and morbidity associated with untreated illness. Understanding the illness and the limitation of our nosology can reduce the gap between having a treatable condition and getting treatment.

What causes misdiagnosis? Surprisingly one of the biggest factors may be the DSM-IV itself. A depressive episode is the initial presentation of BD in more than half of newly-ill patients. Patients having a first episode of depression will be diagnosed as having a unipolar mood disorder until the occurrence of a manic or hypomanic episode. Since operational criteria for episode diagnosis are derived from clinical assessment of signs and symptoms, DSM-IV mood disorder diagnoses do not take age of onset, family history, or course of illness into account. Therefore, identical

33

twins could both have multiple depressive episodes, but if only one had mania they would be diagnosed with different mood disorders.

Improving Diagnostic Confidence

At the end of an evaluation, it is rare that every feature of the history consistently typifies BD or consistently points away from a bipolar diagnosis. Diagnostic confidence can be improved by integrating information gathered across the various dimensions used to validate psychiatric disorders. A bipolarity score which evaluates a patient relative to the traits thought most characteristic of bipolar I disorder can easily be computed. The bipolarity index (*see* Appendix 3) assigns each of these five dimensions a 0–20 score based on the presence of traits most characteristic of bipolar I disorder.

The theoretical case below with the traits most convincing for BD on every dimension would score 100 points.

Episode characteristics:	20 = Documented acute mania or mixed episode with prominent euphoria, grandiosity, or expansiveness, and no significant general medical or known secondary etiology.
Age of onset:	20 = Age 15–19 years.
Course of illness:	20 = Recurrent distinct manic episodes separated by periods of full recovery.
Response to treatment:	20 = Full recovery within four weeks of therapeutic treatment with mood-stabilizing medication.
Family history:	20 = At least one first degree relative with documented bipolar illness.

This rating system transforms bipolarity from a categorical to a continuous dimension and helps to focus the evaluation process.

References

1. Kraepelin E. *Manic-Depressive Insanity and Paranoia*. Edinburgh: E & S Livingstone; 1921.

2. Leonhard K. **Uber monopolare und bipolare endogene Psychosen**. *Nervenarzt* 1968: **39**:104-106.

3. Leonhard K. *Aufteilung der endogenen Psychosen*. Berlin: Akademie; 1957.

4. Angst J, Marneros A. **Bipolarity from ancient to modern times: conception, birth and rebirth.** *J Affect Disord* 2001; **67**:3–19.

5. Winokur G, Clayton P. **Family history studies. I. Two types of affective disorders separated according to genetic and clinical factors.** *Recent Adv Biol Psychiatry* 1966; **9**:35–50.

6. American Psychiatric Association. *Diagnostic and Statistical Manual of Mental Disorders, Fourth Edition.* Washington DC: American Psychiatric Association; 1994.

7. Kessler RC, McGonagle KA, Zhao S et al. **Lifetime and 12-month prevalence of DSM-III-R psychiatric disorders in the United States. Results from the National Comorbidity Survey.** *Arch Gen Psychiatry* 1994; **51**:8–19.

8. Kessler RC, Rubinow DR, Holmes C et al. **The epidemiology of DSM-III-R bipolar I disorder in a general population survey.** *Psychol Med* 1997; **27**:1079–1089.

9. Hantouche EG, Adiskal HS, Lancrenon S et al. **Systematic clinical methodology for validating bipolar-II disorder: data in mid-stream from a French national multi-site study (EPIDEP).** *J Affect Disord* 1998; **50**:163–173.

10. Angst J. Gamma A, Benazzi F et al. **Toward a re-definition of subthreshold bipolarity: epidemiology and proposed criteria for bipolar-II, minor bipolar disorders and hypomania.** *J Affect Disord* 2003; **73**:133–146.

11. Angst J. **The course of affective disorders.** In: *Handbook of Biological Psychiatry.* Van Praag HM and Sachar EJ (Eds). Marcel Dekker, Inc: New York, 1981:225–242.

12. Zis AP, Grof P, Webster M et al. **Prediction of relapse in recurrent affective disorder.** *Psychopharmacol Bull* 1980; **16**:47–49.

13. Roy-Byrne P, Post RM, Uhde TW et al. **The longitudinal course of recurrent affective illness: life chart data from research patients at the NIMH.** *Acta Psychiatr Scand Suppl* 1985; **317**:1–34.

14. Judd LL, Akiskal HS, Schettler PJ et al. **A prospective investigation of the natural history of the long-term weekly symptomatic status of bipolar II disorder.** *Arch Gen Psychiatry* 2003; **60**:261–269.

15. Simon GE, Unutzer J. **Health care utilization and costs among patients treated for bipolar disorder in an insured population.** *Psychiatr Serv* 1999; **50**:1303–1308.

16. Simpson SG, Jamison KR. **The risk of suicide in patients with bipolar disorders.** *J Clin Psychiatry* 1999; **60**(Suppl 2):53–56; discussion 75–76, 113–116.

17. Nilsson A. **Lithium therapy and suicide risk.** *J Clin Psychiatry* 1999; **60**(Suppl):2.

18. Lish JD, Dime Meenan S, Whybrow PC et al. **The National Depressive and Manic-depressive Association (DMDA) survey of bipolar members.** *J Affect Disord* 1994; **31**:281–294.

19. Kessler RC, Stang P, Wittchen HU et al. **Lifetime co-morbidities between social phobia and mood disorders in the US National Comorbidity Survey.** *Psychol Med* 1999; **29**:555–567.

20. Kogan JN, Otto MW, Bauer MS et al. **Demographic and diagnostic characteristics of the first 1000 patients enrolled in the Systematic Treatment Enhancement Program for Bipolar Disorder (STEP-BD).** *Biol Psychiatry* (In Press).

21. Angst F, Stassen HH, Clayton PJ et al. **Mortality of patients with mood disorders: follow-up over 34–38 years.** *J Affect Disord* 2002; **68**:167–181.

22. Nilsson A. **Mortality in recurrent mood disorders during periods on and off lithium. A complete population study in 362 patients.** *Pharmacopsychiatry* 1995; **28**:8–13.

23. Bertelsen A, Harvald B, Hauge M. **A Danish twin study of manic-depressive disorders.** *Br J Psychiatry* 1977; **130**:330–351.

24. Gershon ES. **Genetics of the affective disorders.** *Hosp Pract* 1979; **14**:117–122.

25. Kendler KS, Pedersen NL, Neale MC et al. **A pilot Swedish twin study of affective illness including hospital- and population-ascertained subsamples: results of model fitting.** *Behav Genet* 1995; **25**:217–232.

26. Petronis A. **Epigenetics and bipolar disorder: new opportunities and challenges.** *Am J Med Genet* 2003; **123C**:65–75.

27. Wehr TA. **Sleep-loss as a possible mediator of diverse causes of mania.** *Br J Psychiatry* 1991; **159**:576–578.

28. Ghaemi SN, Sachs GS, Chiou AM et al. **Is bipolar disorder still underdiagnosed? Are antidepressants overutilized?** *J Affect Disord* 1999; **52**:135–144.

29. Baldessarini RJ. **A plea for integrity of the bipolar disorder concept.** *Bipolar Disord* 2000; **2**:3–7.

30. Baldessarini RJ. **Frequency of diagnoses of schizophrenia versus affective disorders from 1944 to 1968.** *Am J Psychiatry* 1970; **127**:759–763.

Chapter 3

Acute Mania Pathway

Introduction

States of pathological mood elevation are accompanied by varying degrees of depressive symptomatology and functional impairment. The fourth edition of the Diagnostic and Statistical Manual (DSM-IV) provides separate criteria for hypomania, mania, and mixed states, but it is difficult to reliably discriminate between these states of mood elevation. Bipolar I patients commonly exhibit a course which fluctuates between these states in a progression which at times is seemingly orderly and at others, chaotic. Therefore, in practical terms, bipolar I patients presenting with hypomanic or mixed episodes can most often be managed appropriately using a common acute mood elevation pathway. Except where otherwise indicated, all statements here concerning treatment for mania should be taken to apply to any episode of mood elevation in a bipolar I patient.

The degree of mood elevation *per se* is neither the decisive factor in the differential diagnosis of hypomanic, manic, and mixed episode, nor is mood elevation the immediate target of treatment. Instead, the degree of impairment and behavioral disturbance as evidenced by aggression, agitation, psychosis, poor judgment, and social or occupational dysfunction is most often the precipitant of clinical attention and hence the primary target of intervention.

The characteristic that most frequently differs between episodes of depression and mood elevation is the variability of the symptoms over time. Even flagrantly manic patients may have hours or days with no overt symptomatology. Since, in many cases, mood elevation is better characterized as a state of hyper-reactivity rather than hyperactivity, assessment in a low stimulus office setting is likely to be unrevealing. This, and the fact that the most common chief complaint during episodes of mania is "depression", makes diagnostic confidence in ruling out the presence of current mania on the basis of brief interviews very low. Careful assessment and collateral sources can reduce the risk of misdiagnosis and mistreatment.

Ideally, treatments which correct the pathophysiology underlying mania would ameliorate all the signs and symptoms associated with pathological mood elevation. As yet there is no truly patholytic therapy available, therefore treatment focuses on restoring behavioral control over the symptoms of acute mania. Typically, for hospitalized patients, symptoms of hyperarousal such as aggression, agitation, restlessness reactivity, and hyper-vigilance are of primary clinical concern.

Evidence from Statistically Valid Studies

The number of agents with class A evidence for acute mania has grown to include lithium, valproate, carbamazepine, and six dopamine-blocking agents (*see* Table 3.1) [1–7]. These treatments with known efficacy should be offered before attempts are made to manage this potentially dangerous condition with unproven alternatives.

Treatments for Acute Mania with Category A Evidence		
	Adequately Powered Placebo-Controlled Clinical Trials	
	Monotherapy	Combination Therapy
Nondopamine-Blocking Agents		
Lithium	Efficacious	Efficacious with antipsychotics
Divalproex	Efficacious	Efficacious with antipsychotics
Carbamazepine	Efficacious	Negative
Gabapentin	Negative	Negative
Topiramate	Negative	Results pending
Dopamine-Blocking Agents		
Olanzapine	Efficacious	Efficacious with lithium or valproate
Ziprasidone	Positive	NA
Risperidone	Positive	Efficacious with lithium or valproate
Haloperidol	Positive	Efficacious with lithium or valproate
Quetiapine	Positive	Efficacious with lithium or valproate
Aripiprazole	Positive	NA

Table 3.1

Taken as a whole, the evidence could be seen to support the utility of dopamine-blocking agents as a class [8]. While this is within what might be considered reasonable, there is no evidence that conventional antipsychotics offer any advantage over atypical agents, except with regards to cost. Studies which directly compare conventional and atypical antipsychotic medications report similar antimanic efficacy but better effectiveness for atypical agents due to better tolerability. Clozapine has been reported to be beneficial for refractory mania, but no controlled data are available [9,10]. For some patients, adjunctive nonspecific treatment targeted at insomnia, restlessness, or anxiety may also be an appropriate means of attaining short-term symptomatic control.

Pathway Overview

The mood elevation pathway offers guidance for the management of any bipolar patient meeting DSM-IV criteria for acute hypomania, mania, or mixed episodes. The first three decision points – diagnostic assessment, ensuring safety, and determination of relative clinical priorities at the start of treatment – lead to the choice of sequential or urgent care as the initial intervention strategy. Treatment is selected from those with established efficacy, and is administered in accordance with the selected strategy (*see* Table 3.2).

For patients nonresponsive after three weeks at the highest tolerated dose, secondary intervention recommendations include use of combined antimanic agents. A substantial evidence base supports combining a nondopamine-blocking agent with a dopamine-blocking drug from among the recognized first-line antimanic medications. Combined use of two nondopamine-blocking antimanic agents, with or without an antipsychotic, is also recommended by several published guidelines, but lacks quality empirical data. Combining multiple dopamine-blocking drugs has not been shown to offer any advantage over monotherapy.

Initiation of Treatment

Following recognition of a new episode of abnormal mood elevation, clinicians face nine basic clinical decisions. The first steps in treatment of mood elevation are to ensure safety, eliminate cycle-promoting agents, and initiate specific antimanic therapies. Along with discontinuing antidepressant medications, consideration should be given to eliminating any other agents which have been implicated as causing mania (eg, steroids, stimulants, sympathomimetics, hormones, muscle relaxants, triazolobenzodiazepines).

Ensuring Safety

Except for the mildest cases, acute manic and mixed episodes warrant hospitalization to ensure safety at the initiation of treatment. Initial medical assessment should rule out causes of secondary mania, with particular emphasis on those that can be life-threatening. The hyperarousal and impulsivity which typifies acute mania poses a serious threat to the patient and those around them. Simple retreat from an uncontrolled high-stimulus environment to the buffered interactions of the hospital often reduces overt expression of symptoms. A state of low symptom expression is a highly desirable context for starting medical treatment, but any lull in acute symptoms is precarious and must not be mistaken for recovery. Staff and family members

Acute Mania Pathway Decision Points		
Decision Point	**Initial Management Recommendations**	
1 Abnormal state with elevated mood warranting treatment	• Assess symptom acuity to determine target symptoms • Review diagnostic criteria, current clinical status, and individual history	
2 Ensure safety	• Choose appropriate treatment venue – acutely manic patients typically require hospitalization • Initiate medical work-up as clinically necessary to rule out life-threatening conditions and common causal factors • Taper and, if possible, eliminate use of substances with known mood-elevating or psychotomimetic effects (eg, antidepressants, stimulants, steroids, substances of abuse)	
3 Determine treatment priority: tolerability versus immediate efficacy	• Review indications for sequential care and urgent care and capacity to maintain acceptable behavioral control within the resources available in the therapeutic venue	
	Sequential care	**Urgent care**
4 Initiate/optimize specific antimanic medications	• Choose lithium, valproate, carbamazepine, or atypical antipsychotic with proven antimanic efficacy	• For combination treatment, select agents with known antimanic efficacy appropriate for aggressive dose titration • Include one dopamine-blocking agent and one nondopamine blocking agent • Valproate and atypical antipsychotics are recommended for use in urgent care
5 Determine need for antipsychotic medication	• Review indications for antipsychotic medication	• Consider conventional antipsychotic agents
6 Determine need for additional antimanic treatment	• Add sequentially as warranted by clinical response to an adequate course, beginning with most tolerable agent not already in use	• Add most efficacious agent not already in use when maximal tolerated doses of current therapeutic regimen have produced no benefit

Table 3.2. Decision points: clinical status = hypomania, mania, or mixed episode. ECT, electroconvulsive therapy.

Acute Mania Pathway Decision Points		
Decision Point	**Sequential care**	**Urgent care**
	• Consider agents with proven antimanic efficacy and/or agents with nonspecific efficacy for targeted problem symptoms (eg, sedatives, hypnotics, anxiolytics)	or insufficient benefit within the period required for onset of action • Consider agents with proven antimanic efficacy and or agents with nonspecific efficacy for targeted problem symptoms (eg, sedatives, hypnotics, anxiolytics)
7 Consider indication for nonstandard interventions	• Review treatment options with putative antimanic efficacy	• Review treatment options with putative antimanic efficacy
8 Determine indication for ECT	• Offer as an option at any time *or* • When two or more adequate trials with agents of known efficacy have proven ineffective *or* • When unable to tolerate adequate pharmacological treatment	• Offer as an option at any time *or* • When combination treatment at maximal tolerable doses has produced no benefit over a period of two weeks or more *or* • When unable to tolerate adequate pharmacological treatment
9 Evaluate continuation in pathway	• Exit if meets criteria for depression or recovered	• Exit if meets criteria for depression or recovered

Table 3.2. *(continued)*

skilled in the arts of avoiding confrontation while redirecting behavior, ignoring provocation where possible, delaying potentially problematic interactions (phone calls from business associates), and distracting from ungratified urges are particularly valuable assets during the lag between initiation of medical treatment and the onset of antimanic effects.

Discharge from the hospital is appropriate once sufficient behavioral control is achieved to allow safe management within the resources available for outpatient treatment. With aggressive treatment, this degree of symptomatic improvement may be achievable within one to four weeks. An additional interval of 12–24 weeks is, however, generally required from the point of initial improvement to achieve a sustained symptomatic recovery from the episode, and full functional recovery is often delayed for longer than one year [11].

Selection of Antimanic Agents

Preference should be given to agents with established antimanic efficacy; therefore, the acute mood elevation pathway (*see* Figure 3.1) begins with either lithium, divalproex, carbamazepine, and/or a dopamine-blocking agent such as aripiprazole,

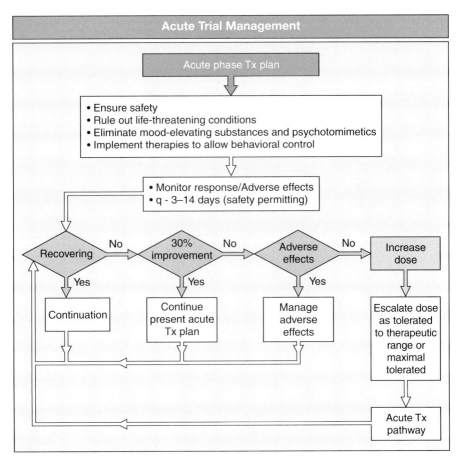

Figure 3.1. Tx, treatment; q - 3–14 days, every 3–14 days.

haloperidol, olanzapine, quetiapine, risperidone, or ziprasidone. Use of these treatments in combination is recommended before moving on to other putative antimanic agents. Electroconvulsive therapy (ECT) has also been reported to be effective treatment for mania and is available for refractory cases and when patient preference or symptom acuity dictate use of the most rapidly effective treatment available. A few reports suggesting worsening of acute mania during treatment with unilateral nondominant ECT provide a rationale for use of bilateral ECT when treating mania.

Sequential Care Strategy

The sequential care strategy is most appropriate when the clinical priority favors tolerability over efficacy. The sequential care approach initially offers as monotherapy the efficacious antimanic agent judged most tolerable for the individual patient.

Benzodiazepines may offer a relatively safe and generally well-tolerated adjunct to the anti-arousal regime, but high doses can lead to counter productive disinhibition.

Urgent Care Strategy

The urgent care strategy is most appropriate when the clinical priority is immediate efficacy. In this approach, efficacious antimanic agents are selected for combination treatment based on their compatibility with a plan for rapid titration to a therapeutic dosage. Based on current data, the urgent care approach recommends combined treatment with a nondopamine-blocking antimanic agent and a dopamine-blocking antimanic agent, or an antipsychotic (dopamine-blocking antimanic) alone. The priority on rapidly attaining therapeutic serum levels makes valproate the preferred nondopamine-blocking agent for urgent care. Atypical antipsychotics and divalproex have the advantage of being generally well tolerated, even when dosed to achieve levels expected to be therapeutic within the first 24 hours

As yet, no category A data have been published demonstrating the benefit of multiple nondopamine-blocking agents or multiple dopamine-blocking antimanic agents.

Menu of Reasonable Choices

The menu of reasonable choices for recommended initial antimanic medication includes three nondopamine-blocking agents (lithium, valproate, carbamazepine), five atypical antipsychotic medications (aripiprazole, olanzapine, quetiapine, risperidone, ziprasidone), and haloperidol. The antimanic properties of other conventional neuroleptics have not been proven, but evidence of a class effect for dopamine-blocking agents is apparent [12]. There is no evidence of a class effect for drugs with anticonvulsant properties.

Defined decision points in the pathway instruct the psychiatrist to consider upward titration for nonresponsive patients every 3–14 days unless adverse effects limit tolerability, or pathway exit criteria are met (*see* Figure 3.2).

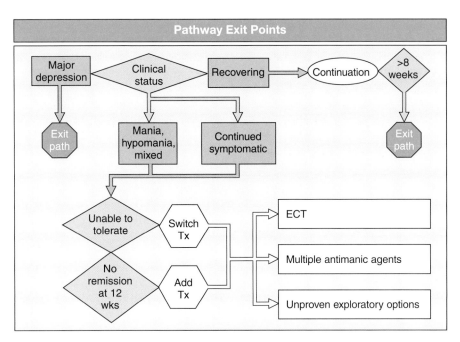

Figure 3.2. ECT, electroconvulsive therapy; Tx, treatment.

Course of Acute-Phase Management

Whichever initial medical treatment is chosen, the goal of titration to therapeutic range is followed by titration to clinical effect at a rate consistent with the selection of the sequential or urgent care strategy. In practice, this means periodic evaluation of progress to determine if further increases should be made in dosing or if additional treatment should be added to the regime. The interval on which progress can be assessed remains a matter of clinical judgment. In the absence of response it may be impractical to delay augmenting the acute treatment regime, but assessing benefit of any treatment based on periods less than one week risks creating a false impression of response as well as nonresponse.

Manic patients typically tolerate reasonably aggressive treatment surprisingly well. When manic symptoms remit, however, complaints of adverse effects increase. In some cases this phenomenon corresponds to alteration in serum drug levels and in others it probably reflects state-dependent variation in perception. In either case, alteration of dose or contra-active intervention is frequently necessary to avoid early rejection of treatment.

Each treatment introduced in the acute phase should be continued with upward titration and monitoring of response every 3–14 days. If the treatment is intolerable or the patient fails to respond to a maximal dose, patients also remain in the acute mania pathway, and the next most attractive treatment on the menu of reasonable choices is added.

Pathway Exit Criteria

Pathway exit criteria link to the next appropriate pathway (eg, relapse prevention, depression). As illustrated in Figure 3.2, patients may remain in the acute mania pathway until reaching criteria for recovery or depression. Patients meeting criteria for depression in the absence of manic symptoms enter the acute depression pathway while continuing antimanic therapies.

Unproven Options: Additional Putative Antimanic Agents

Should first-line agents prove ineffective or unacceptable, the next tier of treatments consists of conventional antipsychotics, clozapine, or other agents with at least one controlled study with an adequate sample indicating efficacy for common target symptoms of mania. Any requirements for slow titration are generally less of a limitation when selecting treatments for refractory mania, where the prospect of a rapid response is desirable but not a necessity. Despite reports of excellent response in refractory patients, concern about bone marrow suppression and the indefinite requirement for blood monitoring limits clozapine's use.

In addition, adrenergic-blocking agents and calcium-channel-blocking agents may be considered, based on small studies which found some agents (clonidine, verapamil) in those classes equivalent to lithium. Uncontrolled case series report an antimanic benefit of cholinomimetics (choline, donepezil), other anticonvulsants (gabapentin, acetazolamide, tiagabine), and other antipsychotics. Given the seriousness of acute mania, these and other nonstandard treatments are best held in reserve for refractory cases or used as adjuncts to treatments with established efficacy (*see* Figure 3.3).

Bipolar II Patients with Current Hypomania

Patients with bipolar II disorder and current hypomania, with no prior history of mania or mixed episodes, may be managed less aggressively and on an outpatient basis. Absence of prior severe episodes does not ensure against progression to mania. The need to watch for impending mania is present in patients with unipolar as well as bipolar mood disorder of all types, but those with bipolar I relatives are thought

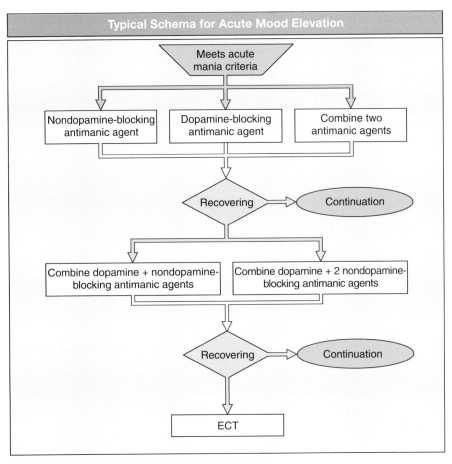

Figure 3.3. ECT, electroconvulsive therapy.

to be most at risk. Warning the patient and significant others about potential signs of progression to mania can create opportunities to truncate impending episodes and avoid the consequences of uncontrolled mania.

Psychosis

Psychosis (hallucinations, delusions, or formal thought disorder) and extreme agitation are clear indications for aggressive treatment. Lithium alone has modest benefit in these cases, and antipsychotics are clearly indicated as part of the initial treatment; these appear to be more rapidly effective than lithium and possibly other putative mood stabilizers. Divalproex has been shown to be as effective as olanzapine for treatment of psychotic mania and (unlike carbamazepine and lamotrigine) can often be titrated rapidly (*see* Table 3.1).

Current Substance Abuse

Current substance abuse is common among patients presenting with acute mania. While in some instances the manic episode may truly be substance induced, this possibility need not delay initiation of antimanic treatment. Patients who remain symptomatic for longer than 72 hours after testing negative for illicit substances are likely to have primary mania. Withdrawal syndromes can also complicate the course of recovery.

The Elderly

Elderly patients may experience intolerance when treated with standard doses of antimanic medications. Antimanic benefit also tends to be achieved at serum levels lower than those required by younger adults.

Pure Euphoric Mania

Pure euphoric mania is unusual and tends to respond best to lithium.

Mania with Depressive Features

Mania with depressive features, short of full depressive episodes, appears more responsive to divalproex or carbamazepine than to lithium. No treatment is clearly superior to placebo for patients with full mixed episodes, but expert opinion favors use of anticonvulsant-type mood stabilizers over lithium. The presence of dysphoria is not an indication for standard antidepressant medication unless the dysphoria persists at least two weeks beyond full resolution of hypomanic symptoms.

References

1. Bowden CL, Brugger AM, Swann AC *et al.* **Efficacy of divalproex vs lithium and placebo in the treatment of mania. The Depakote Mania Study Group.** *JAMA* 1994; **271**:918–924.

2. Sachs GS, Grossman F, Ghaemi SN *et al.* **Combination of a mood stabilizer with risperidone or haloperidol for treatment of acute mania: a double-blind, placebo-controlled comparison of efficacy and safety.** *Am J Psychiatry* 2002; **159**:1146–1154.

3. Tohen M, Sanger TM, McElroy SL *et al.* **Olanzapine versus placebo in the treatment of acute mania. Olanzapine HGEH Study Group.** *Am J Psychiatry* 1999; **156**:702–709.

4. Tohen M *et al.* **Olanzapine versus divalproex sodium for the treatment of acute mania and maintenance of remission: a 47-week study.** *Am J Psychiatry* 2003; **160**:1263–1271.

5. Tohen M, Jacobs TG, Grundy SL *et al.* **Efficacy of olanzapine in acute bipolar mania: a double-blind, placebo-controlled study. The Olanzapine HGGW Study Group.** *Arch Gen Psychiatry* 2000; **57**:841–849.

6. Keck PE Jr, Marcus R, Tourkodimitris S *et al.* **A placebo-controlled, double-blind study of the efficacy and safety of aripiprazole in patients with acute bipolar mania.** *Am J Psychiatry* 2003; **160**:1651–1658.

7. Keck PE Jr, Versiani M, Potkin S *et al.* **Ziprasidone in the treatment of acute bipolar mania: a three-week, placebo-controlled, double-blind, randomized trial.** *Am J Psychiatry* 2003; **160**:741–748.

8. Suppes T, Dennehy EB, Swann AC *et al.* **Report of the Texas Consensus Conference Panel on medication treatment of bipolar disorder 2000.** *J Clin Psychiatry* 2002; **63**:288–299.

9. McElroy SL, Dessain EC, Pope HG *et al.* **Clozapine in the treatment of psychotic mood disorders, schizoaffective disorder, and schizophrenia.** *J Clin Psychiatry* 1991; **52**:411–414.

10. Green AI, Tohen M, Patel JK *et al.* **Clozapine in the treatment of refractory psychotic mania.** *Am J Psychiatry* 2000; **157**:982–986.

11. Tohen M, Hennen J, Zarate CM *et al.* **Two-year syndromal and functional recovery in 219 cases of first-episode major affective disorder with psychotic features.** *Am J Psychiatry* 2000; **157**:220–228.

12. Goodwin GM and the Consensus Group of the British Association for Psychopharmacology. **Evidence-based guidelines for treating bipolar disorder: recommendations from the British Association for Psychopharmacology.** *J Psychopharmacol* 2003; **17**:149–173; discussion 147.

Chapter 4

Bipolar Depression Pathway

Introduction

Treatment of bipolar depression represents the most frequent problem leading bipolar patients to enter healthcare systems, and remains the most common clinical complaint over the entire course of illness [1,2].

The morbidity and mortality associated with bipolar depression present a compelling humanitarian rationale for the administration of aggressive treatment. There are, however, few data demonstrating the benefit of exposing patients to many of the standard antidepressant medications traditionally regarded as first-line interventions for bipolar depression. Naturalistic effectiveness data from the Stanley Research Network and the Systematic Treatment Enhancement Program for Bipolar Disorder (STEP-BD) suggest that only about 15–25% of depressed bipolar subjects treated with a standard antidepressant medication will meet recovery criteria. Furthermore, even among the fortunate minority meeting the recovery criteria, 20–25% relapsed within four months, regardless of whether or not antidepressant medication was continued [3,4].

There is also considerable concern about the potential role of standard antidepressants as an iatrogenic cause of mania and cycle acceleration. Uncontrolled case series suggest that 31–70% of depressed bipolar patients treated with standard antidepressants alone will experience treatment-emergent hypomania or mania, but this risk has never been demonstrated in a rigorous controlled study. In an examination of data from STEP-BD, Truman *et al.* found 19.5% of 1250 retrospectively-reported antidepressant trials were associated with affective switch within the first 12 weeks of treatment. While this report does not establish causality, subjects reporting treatment-emergent affective switch were found to have a significantly higher conditional probability of subsequent treatment-emergent switches, particularly if they were re-exposed to antidepressants of the same class as that associated with the index episode [5].

Pathway Overview

Like the acute mania pathway, the bipolar depression pathway begins with assessment and safety assurance, before progressing to initiation of specific acute-phase treatment.

The risk of self harm and incapacity associated with bipolar depression may require hospitalization until treatment can be safely carried out with the resources available in less restrictive settings. Depending on symptom acuity and therapeutic priorities, specific interventions directed at resolution of the acute symptoms of depression may be initiated using sequential or urgent care strategies. In both cases, each trial should be carried out to a meaningful therapeutic endpoint (*see* below), leading to exit into the relapse prevention pathway, mood elevation pathway, or remaining in the depression pathway for another iteration of acute depression treatment.

Who should have acute phase treatment for depression?

Dysphoria need not meet the criteria for major depression to be dangerous. Treatments with lag times of between two and 12 weeks between initiation and response make little sense for patients with acute episode durations substantially shorter than the exposure time required for onset of antidepressant action.

Supportive strategies which ensure safety at the initiation of treatment are an important component of care even for bipolar patients with long episode durations. Treatment directed at resolution of depression is unlikely to bring substantial relief in less than four weeks and may produce increased motivation and motoric mobilization before impacting the morbid thought process and distorted perceptions that make the depressed state dangerous. Medication prescribed throughout this period prior to expected onset of action should not be presumed to be an adequate intervention unless accompanied by other means of controlling distress (*see* Chapter 7; Suicide Prevention).

Beware of Brief and Biphasic Episodes

The subgroup with well-documented biphasic episodes in which a depressive phase is followed by a manic or mixed phase without an intervening recovery is of particular concern. Naturalistic estimates suggest that 20–40% of bipolar patients diagnosed with depression will be hospitalized or receive outpatient treatment for hypomania or mania within four weeks.

Initiation of Treatment

Following recognition of a new episode of bipolar depression, the treating psychiatrist and patient confront the 14 basic clinical decision points summarized in Table 4.1.

Menu of Reasonable Choices: Selection of an Appropriate Initial Treatment Regimen

A core feature of appropriate initial treatment for bipolar depression is the provision of a regimen with bimodal therapeutic action. When agents with antidepressant activity are dispensed, bipolar patients should also receive protection against further cycling. This means the inclusion of agents with at least some acute or prophylactic antimanic activity. Expert recommendations suggesting use of a "mood stabilizer" as

Bipolar Depression Pathway Decision Points		
Decision Point	**Initial Management Recommendations**	
1 Determine need for acute phase antidepressant treatment	• Review symptom acuity and duration of past episodes of depression	
Ensure safety	• Choose appropriate treatment venue – acutely depressed patients may require hospitalization • Monitor suicidality • Initiate medical work-up as clinically necessary to rule out life-threatening conditions and common causal factors • Taper, and eliminate if possible, use of substances with known depressogenic effects (eg, sedatives, antihypertensives, steroids, substances of abuse)	
2 **Menu of Reasonable Choices:** Determine the most appropriate regimen for acute treatment	**Sequential care**	**Urgent care**
3 Initiate/optimize a treatment plan with bimodal (antidepressant and antimanic/prophylactic) properties	Offer monotherapy treatment with agents with bimodal activity: lamotrigine, lithium, olanzapine, valproate, quetiapine	Offer ECT *or* Offer combination treatment with lamotrigine, lithium, olanzapine, valproate, or quetiapine, or another agent with proven antimanic activity, and an agent with proven efficacy for bipolar depression
4 Determine indication for dopamine-blocking agents (antipsychotic) medication	Review indication for dopamine-blocking agents	
5 Consider psychosocial intervention with evidence of acute efficacy	Determine capacity to participate in CBT or another therapy focused on amelioration of acute symptoms	
6 Offer treatment for comorbid conditions	Encourage abstinence Target anxiety symptoms	
7 Determine indication for adjunctive use of agents proven efficacious for unipolar depression	Review antidepressant menu of reasonable choices	
8 Determine indication for ECT	Review indications for ECT	

Table 4.1. ECT, electroconvulsive therapy; CBT, cognitive-behavioral therapy

	Bipolar Depression Pathway Decision Points	
	Decision Point	**Initial Management Recommendations**
9	Determine indication for nonstandard treatment	Review indications for nonstandard treatments and innovative treatment options
10	Determine appropriate follow-up interval	Schedule follow-up
11	Determine quantity of medication to be dispensed	Review potential for overdose, drug interactions, safety in overdose, and alternatives for dispensing medication
12	Consider addition of maintenance phase treatments in the regimen	See relapse prevention pathway
13	Has the trial reached a therapeutic endpoint?	Titrate dose to achieve recovery, or declare treatment intolerable or ineffective
14	Evaluate continuation in pathway	Exit if meets criteria for: mania, hypomania, mixed or recovered

Table 4.1. *(continued)*

initial treatment for bipolar depression leave many clinicians and patients confused. An unfortunate consequence of using the poorly-defined term "mood stabilizer" is the perception that experts recommend withholding antidepressants from patients diagnosed with depression. The "mood stabilizer" concept originated as a term to convey the bimodal activity of lithium in recognition of its antidepressant as well as antimanic effects. While several medications have demonstrated bimodal acute and/or prophylactic activity, none is equally effective against depression and mania.

Agents with bimodal activity appear to be effective for a substantial proportion of patients with bipolar depression, even when used without standard antidepressant medication. In fact, the only methodologically-sound trial available that compared a mood stabilizer alone to mood stabilizer and antidepressant found no benefit of the combination over lithium alone [6]. Naturalistic data from STEP-BD [4] indicate that response rates for bipolar depression were the same when bimodal agents (mood stabilizers) were used with or without standard antidepressant medication. Although published reports suggest that each of the bimodal agents may be effective, at least in open use, the case for lamotrigine, lithium, olanzapine, and valproate are best supported by evidence.

Over the past five years, five double-blind studies have provided the only available category A data. Calabrese *et al.* [7] reported the superiority of lamotrigine at a daily dose of 50 mg and 200 mg over placebo as a treatment for bipolar depression. Nemeroff *et al.* [6] compared adjunctive treatment with placebo, paroxetine, and imipramine for depressed bipolar patients treated with lithium (serum levels =0.5 mmol/l) and found no significant advantage for either of the standard anti-depressants over placebo. A *post hoc* analysis did, however, reveal an advantage for adjunctive paroxetine in the subgroup of patients with lithium serum levels below 0.8 mmol/l. A 6 g/day dosage of the omega-3 fatty acid, eicosapentaenoic acid (EPA), was no better than placebo in a double-blind trial conducted by the Stanley Foundation Bipolar Network [2]. In the largest bipolar depression study published to date, Tohen *et al.* [8] compared placebo with olanzapine monotherapy, and with combined treatment with olanzapine and fluoxetine. Olanzapine was significantly better than placebo, and the combination of fluoxetine and placebo was statistically superior to olanzapine monotherapy and to placebo. Quetiapine at daily doses of 300 mg and 600 mg was found to be superior to placebo.

Although no head-to-head comparison studies are available, an effect-size analysis – which compares the difference between response rates to placebo and the active treatments, divided by the pooled standard deviation in each trial – does provide a meaningful methodology for comparing treatments across trials. This analysis suggests that comparable antidepressant efficacy for lamotrigine 50 mg, lamotrigine 200 mg, quetiapine 300 mg, quetiapine 600 mg, and combined treatment with olanzapine and fluoxetine (effect size 0.65±0.1) while olanzapine monotherapy appears about half as robust (effect size 0.32).

The literature includes a collection of smaller controlled trials which lack placebo or sufficient sample size to meet the requirements for category A evidence. These studies do, however, offer category C and D evidence in support for the use of electroconvulsive therapy (ECT) and standard antidepressants including bupropion, desipramine, fluoxetine, imipramine, maprotiline, sertraline, tranylcypromine, and venlafaxine. Taken together, this literature suggests that as a broad class, agents efficacious for unipolar depression should be considered as potential second-line adjunctive treatment options for bipolar depression.

Other small controlled trials have reported no difference between a novel anticonvulsant and standard antidepressants or lithium but are impossible to interpret with confidence. Although such reports are widely cited as support for use of carbamazepine, topiramate, and oxcarbazepine, this rationale can only justify use of these agents as potential second-line options pending further study.

Even when not effective as monotherapy, treatment with bimodal agents may have two other potential benefits. First, these agents may (like lithium) reduce the potential risk of affective switch associated with concomitant antidepressant use by approximately 50% [9]. Second, in an analysis of data from the double-blind comparison of maintenance treatment with placebo, lithium and valproate, Gyulai *et al.* reported that when dysphoria prompted the addition of a selective serotonin reuptake inhibitor (SSRI), those maintained on placebo were substantially less successful in averting a full depressive relapse [10]. Thus, the combination of bimodal agents and standard antidepressants appears more robust than standard antidepressants alone.

There is thus some evidence to support expert consensus recommendations to use a bimodal agent ("mood stabilizer") in every phase of the illness and to avoid monotherapy with standard antidepressants. When standard antidepressant medications are prescribed, the co-administration of lithium, lamotrigine, valproate, olanzapine, quetiapine, or another agent with antimanic properties is always recommended.

Sequential Care Strategy

Over the first three weeks of treatment, in the majority of cases, it is reasonable to offer patients with mild–moderate bipolar depression a single agent with bimodal activity ("mood stabilizer" medications). If the patient is not substantially improved at that point, sequential addition of standard antidepressants or ECT should be offered unless contraindicated based on individual history.

Urgent Care Strategy

For the most severely-ill patients, ECT should be offered as the safest, fastest, and most effective acute treatment available. When this is unacceptable or when tolerability and risk of mania are not of paramount clinical priority, treatment can be initiated with a bimodal agent and a standard antidepressant. Depressed bipolar patients with psychosis, acute suicidal intent, or severe agitation are excellent candidates for ECT, but may find it more acceptable to begin an alternative urgent care strategy with a combination of bimodal agents, a standard antidepressant, and a dopamine-blocking agent.

Selection of Treatments with Specific Antidepressant Efficacy

Based on data from unipolar depression, the efficacy of approved standard antidepressant medications appears equivalent overall [11] and all could be considered for use in treatment of bipolar depression. In constructing the menu of reasonable choices, antidepressant drugs with the most desirable adverse effect profile (likelihood of serious adverse effects = very low; tolerability of expectable adverse effects = very high) could be considered as potential first-line antidepressant therapy. A menu of reasonable choices for individual cases would be selected from this subset, based on the prior treatment history, specific contraindications (allergy, cardiac status, insurance restrictions, cost, safety in overdose), tolerability concerns, and preferences of each patient.

ECT and those treatments with mechanisms of action similar to that of first-line agents but with somewhat less desirable adverse-effects profiles are designated "available if preferred".

Course of Acute-Phase Management

Each acute-phase trial initiated should be carried out to reach a meaningful thera-peutic endpoint: full response, intolerance, or nonresponse. Partial response should be considered a tentative evaluation, subject to more definitive reinterpretation in light of further experience at a higher dose or longer treatment duration. The goal of follow-up visits during the acute phase is to monitor response and manage adverse effects. Figure 4.1 illustrates decision making over a typical course of acute treatment. When patients present with remission of depression it is appropriate to offer contin-uation treatment (*see* Chapter 1). Similarly, it may be wisest to make no changes in the treatment of patients with substantial improvement (>30%) even though their clinical status remains "depressed" or "continued symptomatic".

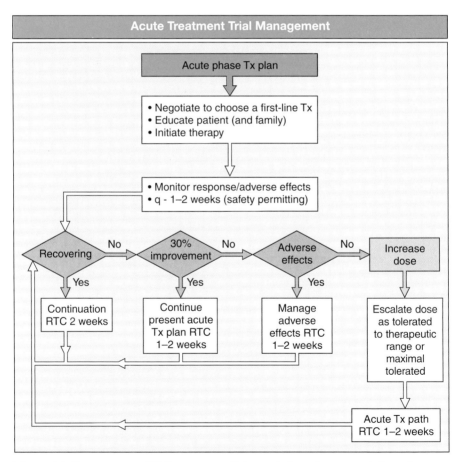

Figure 4.1. Tx, treatment; RTC, return to clinic; q - 1–2 weeks, every 1–2 weeks.

Reports from Nierenberg *et al.* [12] suggest a progressively lower conditional probability of response given no significant improvement after two, four, six, and eight weeks of treatment at a given dose of antidepressant medication. Therefore, patients experiencing no significant improvement and tolerating treatment without significant adverse effects are candidates for upward dose titration until reaching maximal tolerated doses. When adverse effects preclude increasing dosage, titration is delayed or dosage may be decreased to allow management of adverse effects. If these tactics do not succeed in allowing an adequate treatment trial, alternative treatment may be required. For patients with clear worsening, it is reasonable to cut a trial short and move on to an alternative treatment, especially if concern arises that treatment has contributed to the increased dysphoria or worsening of suicidal ideation. Otherwise, patients should be encouraged to sustain treatment for at least six weeks at an adequate dose in order to fairly evaluate a treatment trial.

Transition to continuation treatment begins when a clinical status of "recovering" is assigned, but the transition from recovering to recovered seldom occurs smoothly. For most patients, the early months typically include weeks in which the assigned clinical status will be "continued symptomatic" or "depression". Such "relapses" are to be expected and when persistent may indicate a need for further titration of acute phase treatment.

Indications for Nonstandard Treatments

The availability of standard agents with differing structure, adverse-effect profiles, and mechanisms of action provides a long list of options, which can be confidently offered before turning to nonstandard treatments. There is little to be gained, however, by forbidding the use of adjuncts such as acupuncture, homeopathy, or dietary supplements with no known contraindication. Exploration of these treatments and response should also be tracked in the patient's chart.

Determining the Indication for ECT

ECT may be appropriate at any time, including as an initial treatment when dictated by symptom acuity or patient preference, and all patients should be made aware of the availability of this therapy. ECT may be encouraged as an early option for acutely suicidal, psychotic, catatonic, or severely-depressed patients but is generally held in reserve for patients intolerant of, or refractory to, mood stabilizers and standard antidepressant medications. Ethical considerations suggest that all patients refractory to standard bimodal agents in combination with standard antidepressants be made aware of ECT as a treatment option.

Determining the Indication for Antipsychotic Medication

Patients with delusions, hallucinations, and severe agitation often benefit from adjunctive antipsychotic medications. Atypical antipsychotic medication may improve some symptoms of depression, but there are not, as yet, sufficient data to conclude that, as a class, these agents have antidepressant properties, or to be confident in assessing how these agents compare to standard antidepressant medications. Neuroleptic medications, particularly at high dosage, can increase dysphoria in some patients.

Determining the Follow-Up Interval

Local standards and clinician judgment determine acceptable intervals for follow-up. In most circumstances, when new medical treatment is initiated, a follow-up interval of one to two weeks is appropriate for managing most outpatients. Patients with mild–moderate depression and good support systems may be more safely managed at longer intervals than severely-ill patients who lack reliable supports, but all depressed patients are at risk of self-destructive behavior. In the absence of reliable predictors of danger, it makes sense to evaluate both the inclination and opportunity for self harm. Patients with active suicidal ideation or other signs of high inclination warrant aggressive treatment aimed at reducing the depression, and may require hospitalization, since none of the currently available antidepressant treatments for outpatients deliver reliable results in less than three weeks. If measures are taken to adequately monitor the patient and reduce opportunities for self harm (eg, eliminate access to firearms and other lethal agents), many acutely-depressed patients can be managed without hospitalization. Accordingly, it is best to initiate treatment with a follow-up interval which avoids dispensing large amounts of potentially lethal medications (especially lithium and tricyclic antidepressants).

Determining the Quantity of Medication to be Dispensed

Depression is a risk factor for suicide even in patients evidencing no current self-destructive urges. Limiting the quantity of medication prescribed at any one time to amounts which would not be lethal if the entire amount dispensed were ingested, does not by itself assure safety, but can lessen one potential source of lethality. Dispensing amounts of medication sufficient to ensure supply to the next appointment may require extra safety measures.

Endpoints

As illustrated in Figures 4.1 and 4.2, acute-phase treatment continues unless the patient experiences affective switch (hypomania, mania, mixed episode) or recovery. Patients unable to tolerate an effective dosage or unresponsive to a full trial of maximal dose are offered acute treatment with another standard antidepressant, ECT, and innovative treatment (depending on their symptom acuity and history of prior response).

Before concluding that a treatment is ineffective, some experts recommend augmentation strategies such as lithium, thyroid stimulants, or neurotransmitter precursors in an effort to potentiate standard treatments. The benefit of these agents is not well established, but augmentation strategies may be beneficial even if their usefulness is limited to sustaining therapeutic optimism long enough to complete a 16-week therapeutic trial with the highest tolerated dose of a standard agent.

Management of affective switch begins with discussing the risk of switch and warning signs with patients and family members. There are no data to guide management of affective switch, but reduction or elimination of antidepressant

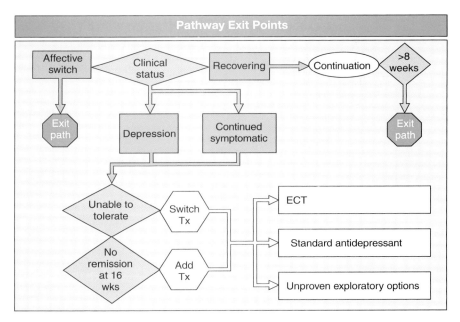

Figure 4.2. Tx, treatment; ECT, electroconvulsive therapy.

medication may be sufficient management in some mild cases. Treatment is otherwise the same as for primary hypomania or mania.

Considerations for Special Subpopulations

Treatment-Naive Bipolar I and Bipolar II Patients

The subpopulation of treatment-naive BP I and BP II patients includes a substantial proportion of patients with a good prognosis who are likely to respond well to bimodal agents. Patients with a history of prior treatment suffering a recurrence during an interval in which they received no prophylactic treatment are also frequently responsive to mood stabilizer treatment.

Breakthrough Episodes

Patients with breakthrough episodes occurring during ongoing maintenance treatment appear to be less treatment responsive, particularly if the breakthrough occurred while receiving therapeutic levels of lamotrigine, lithium, valproate, olanzapine, or carbamazepine. Such patients may, however, respond to an increased dose of their prophylactic treatment aimed at improving the antidepressant benefit of bimodal agents, particularly if their medication was maintained at suboptimal levels (lithium <0.8 mmol/L, lamotrigine <200 mg/day, valproate <80 µg/ml, olanzapine 10 mg/day, or carbamazepine < 8.0 µg/ml).

Breakthrough episodes occurring during the course of prophylaxis with bimodal agents and standard antidepressants may represent an even more refractory subgroup but might also include some cases in which the course of illness was driven by the antidepressant itself. For these patients, recommendations for acute treatment follow the same guideline (increase dose or add a new antidepressant) but following appropriate continuation treatment, unsuccessful acute treatments and those ineffective prophylactically would be tapered in the maintenance phase. Careful record keeping is necessary to ascertain the effect of those treatments that are sustained in the maintenance phase.

Patients with a history of treatment-emergent affective switch or rapid cycling are at highest risk of experiencing treatment-emergent switch or cycle acceleration when treated with standard antidepressants.

References

1. Judd LL, Akiskal HS, Schettler PJ *et al.* **A prospective investigation of the natural history of the long-term weekly symptomatic status of bipolar II disorder.** *Arch Gen Psychiatry* 2003; **60**:261–269.

2. Post RM, Leverich GS, Altshuler LL *et al.* **An overview of recent findings of the Stanley Foundation Bipolar Network (Part I).** *Bipolar Disord* 2003; **5**:310–319.

3. Altshuler L, Suppes T, Black D *et al.* **Impact of antidepressant discontinuation after acute bipolar depression remission on rates of depressive relapse at 1-year follow-up.** *Am J Psychiatry* 2003; **160**:1252–1262.

4. Sachs GS. *STEP-BD Update: What have we learned. in International Bipolar Disorder.* 2003. Pittsburgh, PA: Western Psychiatric Institute and Clinic, UPMC Health System.

5. Truman APA poster 2003.

6. Nemeroff CB, Evans DL, Gyulai L *et al.* **Double-blind, placebo-controlled comparison of imipramine and paroxetine in the treatment of bipolar depression.** *Am J Psychiatry* 2001; **158**:906–912.

7. Calabrese JR, Bowden CL, Sachs GS *et al.* **A double-blind placebo-controlled study of lamotrigine monotherapy in outpatients with bipolar I depression. Lamictal 602 Study Group.** *J Clin Psychiatry* 1999; **60**:79–88.

8. Tohen M, Vieta E, Calabrese J *et al.* **Efficacy of olanzapine and olanzapine-fluoxetine combination in the treatment of bipolar I depression.** *Arch Gen Psychiatry* 2003; **60**:1079–1088.

9. Prien RF, Kupfer DJ, Mansky PA *et al.* **Drug therapy in the prevention of recurrences in unipolar and bipolar affective disorders. Report of the NIMH Collaborative Study Group comparing lithium carbonate, imipramine, and a lithium carbonate-imipramine combination.** *Arch Gen Psychiatry* 1984; **41**:1096–1104.

10. Gyulai L, Bowden CL, McElroy SL *et al.* **Maintenance efficacy of divalproex in the prevention of bipolar depression.** *Neuropsychopharmacology* 2003; **28**:1374–1382.

11. Frank E, Karp JF, Rush AJ. **Efficacy of treatments for major depression.** *Psychopharmacol Bull* 1993; **29**:457–475.

12. Nierenberg AA, McLean NE, Alpert JE *et al.* **Early nonresponse to fluoxetine as a predictor of poor 8-week outcome.** *Am J Psychiatry* 1995; **152**:1500–1503.

Chapter 5

Relapse Prevention Pathway

Introduction

Relapse prevention is the primary focus of the maintenance phase of treatment. When a patient has "recovered", treatment objectives shift from those related to resolution of acute symptoms to preventing recurrences and maximizing the patient's quality of life.

Pathway Overview

The relapse prevention pathway divides the maintenance phase into two parts: an early initiation phase and a later monitoring phase. During the initiation phase the decision points involve determining whom to treat and selection of the treatment regime. In the monitoring phase, follow-up care focuses on the routine management of the therapeutic regime, detection of potential impending episodes, and interventions to sustain remission.

Determining who Should have Maintenance Treatment?

The question of who should have maintenance treatment generates considerable academic debate, but has little practical significance in clinical practice. At the time of diagnosis of bipolar disorder (BD), patients tend to have already experienced more than three episodes, and even under the most conservative guidelines would be considered appropriate candidates for maintenance treatment.

Many experts recommend maintenance treatment for all patients who have suffered even a single acute manic episode, while others feel it is appropriate to reserve long-term maintenance treatment for patients who have experienced two or more manic episodes. The former point out the 95% lifetime risk of recurrence after a single manic episode, and refer to studies that have shown a loss of acute and prophylactic benefit (at least of lithium) among patients with as few as three episodes. The latter point out that the median duration of remission following the first acute episode is more than four years and highlight the paucity of evidence justifying chronic treatment for bipolar patients beyond 32 weeks [1].

Another aspect of selecting patients for maintenance treatment relates to the likelihood that patients will discontinue treatment regardless of the psychiatrist's recommendations. Patients who discontinue lithium treatment, particularly when discontinuation is abrupt, appear to be at increased risk for recurrence. Goodwin and colleagues have attempted to quantify the risks and benefits of lithium maintenance and recommend against offering maintenance treatment to patients judged unlikely or unwilling to adhere to treatment for at least two years [2]. It is unclear when in the course of treatment the liability to such discontinuation phenomena develops or if similar phenomena apply to other maintenance treatments [3–5]. In a large prospective study, Bowden *et al.* found no evidence of discontinuation phenomena following discontinuation of acute treatment with lithium or divalproex [6,7].

Such debate has little relevance to clinical decision making for the majority of bipolar patients. Many clinical experts recommend continuation of effective acute-phase treatments for a period of one year beyond the onset of clinical remission, and a substantial proportion of bipolar patients relapse within this period of prudent continuation treatment [8]. Another distinct subgroup receives long-term care in the context of chronic illness [9–11]. A surprisingly large proportion of patients chronically fluctuate between full syndromal states and periods of subsyndromal acute symptoms during which any remissions are too brief to meet the "recovered" criteria and the cycle length is too long to meet criteria for rapid cycling [12–17]. Although these chronically ill subjects never achieve the period of sustained euthymia considered a prerequisite to consideration of discontinuing acute-phase treatments, it is appropriate to treat these patients in a manner similar to that described in the rapid cycling pathway, in which relapse prevention is a target treatment objective along with the acute treatment strategies.

The clinician should exercise caution, and be aware that meeting the operational criteria for a clinical status of "recovered" does not always mean that treatment was effective. The maintenance phase is defined as beginning after a remission meeting criteria for "recovered". Therefore, a status of "recovered" is often interpreted as an indication that the pathophysiology underlying the acute episode has been corrected and the patient has returned to a normal well state. It is worth remembering, however, that this interpretation is only one of several plausible explanations. An observed remission of symptoms could represent three distinctly different conditions:

1. remission sustained by the effects of ongoing acute treatment;

2. a return to the well state in which improvement is attributed to reaching the endpoint of the acute episode; or

3. transient apparent remission during the period of low amplitude symptoms encountered around the inflection point in the progression between polar extremes.

The first represents a clinical state for which continued acute-phase management is needed (like continuing use of an umbrella while walking in a rainstorm). The second, "recovered", state may or may not be due to treatment effects *per se* (like when the rain has stopped, but we don't know if the route traveled shortened exposure to the storm) but would be appropriately managed in accordance with the priorities of the maintenance phase (*see* Chapter 1). The last – a transient phase of apparent remission (like passing through the eye of a hurricane) – during which the patient might be assigned a status of recovering or recovered (depending on its duration), and the improvement attributed to the last intervention. In the context of long-term mood charting, the latter pattern can be recognized as signifying only the unmodi-fied autonomous progression of phases in the course of continuous cycling. Thus, it is not possible to attribute a recovery to treatment with complete confidence, and apparently effective treatments can appear to lose efficacy over the course of long-term treatment.

The longer the duration of a remission, the more likely it is that a transition has been made from "recovering" to a true "recovered" state. The designation "recovered" – defined as eight or more consecutive weeks with two or moderate symptoms – is a widely-used if somewhat arbitrary convention. In the absence of longitudinal indi-vidual experience, an eight-week remission provides a standard reference point sug-gesting a durable remission has occurred due to treatment or because the natural endpoint of the previous episode has been passed.

The eight-week convention can, however, be ignored when accumulated individ-ual experience over the course of multiple episodes demonstrates a pattern of much longer or shorter duration. Such individual experience is, at present, the best guidance for decisions about when to shift from continuation to maintenance-phase treatment.

The available literature provides valuable, albeit very incomplete, guidance to the clinician attempting to match individual bipolar patients with prophylactic treat-ment strategies. Therefore, the process of sustaining remission and maximizing qual-ity of life is most likely to be successful if, over the course of years, the outcome of each intervention is carefully evaluated so as to inform the iterative development of an individualized treatment plan. A careful review of the patient's history is the best available way to determine the most appropriate regimen for prophylaxis. Once a stable regimen has been established, relapse prevention relies on a schedule of rou-tine follow-up in which the primary objectives are monitoring the treatment regimen, managing adverse effects, managing comorbid conditions, and monitoring for early clinical signs and symptoms that may herald an impending episode. Systematic record keeping facilitates meeting these objectives.

Initiation of Treatment

The question of which bipolar patients should receive maintenance treatment is an important one. While the present literature does not entirely resolve this issue, from a practical point of view the areas of agreement extend to three large groups:

1. patients with more than two prior episodes;

2. patients who experience a breakthrough episode during the first year of treatment following an acute episode; and

3. chronically ill and long cycle-length patients who do not achieve a remission of acute symptoms sufficient to meet the criteria for "recovered".

Determining the Most Appropriate Regimen for Prophylaxis

After successful acute- and continuation-phase treatment, the question of appropriate prophylaxis will be determined by the patient's history and response to prior treatment trials.

The sequential strategy aim of monotherapy is a reasonable starting point for many patients and will result in the gradual tapering of acute-phase treatments and the optimization or initiation of a treatment with proven prophylactic benefit. A history of rapid recurrence following tapering of acute-phase treatment should prompt consideration of prolonged use of therapy (*see* caution above). There is, however, little reason to rush the tapering of successful acute-phase treatments, and a gradual (20–33%/month) dosage reduction appears less likely to precipitate problems than an abrupt discontinuation.

Aim for an Optimal Short-Term Course of Treatment

The clinician should aim for an optimal short-term course of treatment sufficient to evaluate potential benefits and adverse effects. For those who attain full recovery after a first manic or hypomanic episode it is likely to be more productive to stress the importance of maintaining treatment throughout the period of highest risk – the first 24–32 weeks following remission – rather than soliciting a lifetime commitment to prophylactic treatment. Since the outcome during this period will be an important guide in the planning of future maintenance treatment, patients should be encouraged to view the first six to nine months of treatment as a therapeutic probe to evaluate the potential benefit of a given treatment. As such, it can be helpful to stress the importance of consistent dosing during this trial period to avoid wasting time or casting aside potentially beneficial treatments due to a suboptimal therapeutic trial. Patients assured that their subjective evaluation of the benefit:adverse effects ratio will be respected will often accept a therapeutic trial knowing that they are not committed to continue treatment with no benefit or intolerable side effects. Table 5.1 can be used to aid this discussion.

Evidence from Statistically Valid Studies

High-quality relapse prevention data are scant, largely because of the inherent difficulties in the design and ethical conduct of the large-scale longitudinal studies required. There is no agreement about the optimal design for relapse-prevention studies, nor is there a single outcome measure that can be used across all aspects of maintenance treatment. True maintenance studies, in which patients who have

Short Term Evaluation of Intervention				
	Benefit			
Adverse Effects + Expense	**None**	**Fair**	**Good**	**Excellent**
None	Δ	?	+	+
Mild	Δ	?	?	?
Moderate	Δ	?	?	?
Severe	Δ	Δ	?	?

Table 5.1. Δ, change treatment; +, continue treatment; ?, continue or change based on patient preference.

recovered from acute episodes are randomly assigned to start active treatment or placebo, are not available, and much of the available data are contaminated by the effect of abrupt discontinuation of prior treatments. The ideal treatment would prevent episodes both of depression and mania, restore full premorbid function, and have no intolerable adverse effects. Although lithium is without question the best-studied agent, prior to 2000 there were no randomized, parallel group trials of this therapy, and many of the previous reports lacked rigorous methodology. Since 2000, category A relapse-prevention data have become available supporting the use of divalproex, lamotrigine, lithium, and olanzapine for at least one relapse-prevention outcome measure [7]. The first such study, by Bowden et al., found no significant benefit of lithium or divalproex over placebo for prevention of mania or depression considered separately. Considering overall relapse into an episode of any kind, however, divalproex did prevent significantly more episodes than placebo. The absence of prophylactic benefit against mania in that trial for lithium as well as divalproex was unexpected, and in light of the low relapse rates in the placebo-treated group, might be understood as an unintended consequence of the placebo-controlled design. The possibility of randomization to placebo most likely discouraged entry of subjects at high risk for relapse. In two placebo-controlled comparisons with lamotrigine, lithium was more effective than placebo in preventing episodes of any kind, and specifically in preventing manic recurrences, but the trend for prevention of depressive episodes did not reach statistical significance [18,19].

Conversely, lamotrigine was more effective than placebo overall (preventing depression and mania) and specifically in preventing depressive episodes, but the trend for prevention of mania did not reach statistical significance [18,19]. Differences between lamotrigine and lithium did not reach statistical significance on any efficacy measure; however, tremor, sedation, and gastrointestinal side effects were more common in the lithium-treated group.

Olanzapine has been found more effective than lithium in prevention of manic recurrence but not significantly different for prevention of depression [20]. There is also evidence of fewer episodes in patients given combined treatment with olanzapine plus lithium or valproate compared to placebo plus lithium or valproate (*see* Table 5.2).

Treatments for Relapse Prevention with Category A Evidence		
Adequately Powered Placebo-Controlled Clinical Trials		
Prevent/Delay Manic Recurrence Episode	**Prevent/Delay Depressive Recurrence Episode**	**Prevent/Delay any Recurrence**
Lithium — Efficacious in 2 of 3 trials	NS	Efficacious in 2 of 3 trials
Divalproex — NS	NS	Efficacious in 1 trial
Lamotrigine — NS	Efficacious	Efficacious 2 trials
Olanzapine — Efficacious	NS	Efficacious 2 trials

Table 5.2. NS, nonsignificant.

Expert guidelines recommend reserving the use of novel agents to those cases with unsatisfactory response to trials of proven treatments alone and in combination. Since a substantial proportion of bipolar patients will not have adequate response to well-studied therapies, knowledge of other putative and innovative treatment modalities is essential. Suppes reported an open randomized comparison of adding treatment to the ongoing treatment regime of symptomatic bipolar patients. A significant advantage was found for clozapine over clinician choice of another adjunctive treatment excluding clozapine [21].

Sequential Care versus Urgent Care

The concepts of sequential care and urgent care also apply to maintenance-phase treatment strategies, and sequential care may be appropriate for many subjects. After education regarding the need for treatment and accurate information about possible adverse effects of each option on the menu of reasonable choices, subjects without a history of breakthrough episodes (especially those with few and/or mild episodes or long cycle lengths) can be offered a choice of any intervention with positive category A evidence for use as monotherapy maintenance treatment. When prevention of breakthrough manic or mixed episodes is of greatest clinical concern, the best evidence supports initiation of treatment with lithium or an atypical antipsychotic. The evidence favors lamotrigine when prevention of depression is the highest clinical priority.

The use of durable educational materials that can be taken from the office and shared with supports and documentation in the chart of the treatment selection process is recommended.

Patients frequently exercise their right to reject these first-line recommendations because they disagree with the need for prophylactic treatment or fear potential adverse effects. Regardless of the reason for rejecting the first-line agents, rational alternative therapies can and should be offered after documentation of the fact that first-line options were rejected.

Differentiating Discordance and Noncompliance

Concordance – agreement between doctor and patient about the best treatment plan – is an important long-term treatment goal. Over time, discordance about the selection of treatment and lifestyle issues can be addressed in light of recorded outcomes. Repeating failed plans is difficult to justify and over time the iterative process sequenced in accordance with patient preferences eventually yields benefits. Patients are, however, frequently concordant with the plan, but for a variety of illness-related or practical reasons, attempts to carry out the plan are thwarted by noncompliance. In such cases, management stressing the needs for external aides to compliance with the patient's plan are often more effective than repeated finger pointing. The difficulties of consistent dosing can be lessened by use of medication-taking routines, pill dispensers, single daily dosing, attention to adverse effects, support involvement, and in some cases long-acting injectable medications [22] or ECT [23].

When breakthrough episodes have occurred, the sequential approach includes selection of an alternative monotherapy or the introduction of additional agents for combined prophylactic use. It is appropriate to discontinue treatments that have failed due to lack of efficacy or intolerance.

The urgent care approach uses two main tactics, multiple prophylactic medications and continuation of successful acute-phase treatments.

Relapse Prevention Pathway Decision Points

The treatment plan for the maintenance phase should take into account the many factors implicated in triggering recurrences (see Table 5.3). Expert recommendations recognize both the essential role of "mood stabilizing" medications and the benefit of psychosocial interventions (including formal psychotherapies, patient/family education, and self-help groups) in treatment plans aimed at preventing relapse.

Paradoxically, the first decision point in relapse prevention typically occurs during the acute phase (see Table 5.4). Somatic therapies that will comprise maintenance-phase

Common Triggers for Affective Instability		
Sleep loss		
Alcohol/substance abuse or withdrawal		
EEG abnormality		
Hypothyroidism		
Migraine headache		
Nicotine withdrawal		
Rapid discontinuation of lithium		
Antidepressants	Use	
	Discontinuation	
Other medications	Steroids	Anabolic steroids
		Glucocorticoids
	Sympathomimetics	Stimulants, caffeine, decongestants, bronchodilators, anorectics
	Reproductive hormones/blockers	Gonadotropins
		Oral contraceptives
		Testosterone
		DHEA
		Lupron®
		Clomiphene
		Tamoxifen
	Muscle relaxants	
	Triazolobenzodiazepines	
	Treatment for Parkinson's disorder	
	Thyroxine	
	Barbiturates	
Interpersonal	Conflict/trauma	
	Grief	
	Success	
	Loss of support systems	
	Circadian disruptions	
	Seasonality	
	East-West travel	
	Shift work	

Table 5.3. DHEA, dehydroepiandrosterone; EEG, electroencephalogram.

treatment are usually initiated during the acute phase of treatment. Therefore, the goal of enhanced protection against recurrence places a maintenance-phase decision point in the acute phase by influencing the choice of acute treatment strategies. That is to say that during the acute phase of mixed, manic, or depressive episodes, treatment strategies are implemented which lay the foundation for relapse prevention. Sometimes, as in the case of a patient with breakthrough mania during lithium prophylaxis, the addition of valproate targets prophylaxis as well as acute symptoms. Similarly, the strategy of

Relapse Prevention Pathway Decision Points		
Decision Point	**Initial Management Recommendations**	
Initiation		
1 Determine need for maintenance phase treatment	Review past symptom acuity and cycle frequency	
2 Determine the most appropriate regimen for prophylaxis	**Sequential care**	**Urgent care**
Consider which acute phase treatments will be included in the maintenance regimen	Attempt monotherapy maintenance with an agent of proven efficacy Review prior attempts to tapering Antimanic agents Antidepressants Anxiolytics Psychosocial interventions	Combine efficacious therapies Consider prolonged use of successful acute-phase treatments
Optimize/add prophylactic anticycling agents	Replace: previous ineffective treatment with lamotrigine, lithium, valproate, or olanzapine if not already present Consider appropriate psychotherapy	Add: lamotrigine, lithium, valproate, or olanzapine if not already present Consider appropriate psychotherapy
3 Offer treatment for comorbid conditions	Encourage abstinence Target anxiety symptoms	
4 Taper any acute phase treatment gradually	20–33% per month	
5 Determine appropriate follow-up interval	Assess every 1–2 months depending on changes made to treatment	
Monitoring		
6 Manage adverse effects	Actively elicit Intervene for weight gain >2 kg (5 lb) Offer alternatives when bothersome side effects occur	
7 Maintain prophylactic treatments in target range	Monitor compliance and aim for therapeutic serum level if range known	
8 Monitor for roughening	Raise dose of prophylactic treatments Decrease follow-up interval	
9 Evaluate outcome on course of illness	Use systematic assessment and prospective charting to determine if completely effective, partially effective or ineffective	

Table 5.4

Relapse Prevention Pathway Decision Points	
Monitoring	
– Add additional anticycling agent(s)	See menu of putative anticycling agents
– Eliminate ineffective agents	Avoid exotic polypharmacy. Gradually taper if no benefit after 6 months or 3 cycle lengths
10 Management of next acute episode	Review performance of each element in the previous treatment plan. Consider maintenance phase options when selecting acute phase treatments

Table 5.4. (*continued*)

discontinuing standard antidepressant medication during a manic episode may be chosen with an eye towards enhancing protection against future recurrences. In other circumstances, as when attempts to taper antipsychotics or antidepressants are followed by relapse, historical evidence supports incorporating therapies usually limited to the acute and continuation phase into the maintenance regimen [24].

Other Agents: Avoid Undisciplined Exotic Polypharmacy

The chronic recurrence that typifies BD can result in a progressive increase in the number of medications used [25]. While this may lead to the finding of an effective regimen, it can be dangerous as well as expensive and clinically confusing. Avoid the pitfalls of polypharmacy by carefully tracking interventions over a reasonable therapeutic trial. Discontinue treatments when the record reflects no evidence of a benefit.

Treatments other than those currently considered to be "mood stabilizers" or approved for prophylactic use may well be appropriate for some patients. Generally, however, it is prudent to consider a gradual tapering of acute-phase medications such as standard antidepressants and antipsychotics, which might have been part of the acute regimen. Treatment with antidepressants has been associated with increased cycle frequency [26–28] and the induction of rapid cycling [29]. Neuroleptics have often been used during the maintenance phase, despite concern about tardive dyskinesia and data showing that maintenance treatment with flupenthixol resulted in more frequent depressions than maintenance with placebo [30]. There are as yet no double-blind controlled data for atypical antipsychotic medications.

Case reports have raised concern that atypical antipsychotics can induce mania, but this phenomena is consistently absent in prospective double-blind trials [31,32].

Special Populations

Breakthrough During Tapering

Patients suffering relapse during the course of tapering may be appropriate candidates for chronic treatment with antipsychotic or antidepressant medications.

Following Mixed Episodes

Since the treatment recommendations for patients with mixed episodes are the same as those in the mania pathway, most patients with mixed episodes will have tapered their antidepressant medication. Data from the National Institute of Mental Health (NIMH) collaborative study suggest maintaining treatment with standard antidepressants following resolution of mixed episodes is particularly risky [33]. However, antidepressants may be reintroduced for those patients with persistent depression following resolution of the manic component of the mixed episode. In such cases, a slow tapering of standard antidepressant is recommended following an appropriate continuation phase.

Following Electroconvulsive Therapy

Patients responding to acute treatment with ECT can be divided into subgroups based on whether ECT was used as a matter of choice (eg, symptom acuity warranted aggressive treatment) or because the acute episode proved refractory to other somatic interventions [34]. In either case, early relapse is common following abrupt discontinuation of ECT. In all cases, mood stabilizing medications should be offered for prophylaxis, and in the latter case, consideration should be given to use of ECT as a maintenance treatment [23,35,36].

Women Seeking to Conceive

Bipolar illness is not an absolute contraindication to child bearing. When bipolar women and their spouses seek counseling prior to conception, a review of the teratogenic potential of the treatment is necessary as well as the risk of relapse during gestation and the postpartum period. Generally, most experts recommend delaying attempts to conceive until patients have enjoyed a stable remission of at least six to twelve months. Selection of a treatment strategy for bipolar women with stable remission should take into account the severity and frequency of prior episodes, age of the patient, and the quality of available supports. A range of management options should be reviewed, allowing individual patients and their spouses to choose the risks most acceptable. Older women or those with more severe episodes may choose to conceive while maintaining treatment and use fetal ultrasound or amniocentesis to screen for potential teratogenic effects. Younger women and those with milder illness may more reasonably plan to taper some or all medication prior to conception while relying on nonpharmacological strategies at least through the first trimester. Consultation with psychopharmacologists, gynecologists, or pediatricians familiar with the issues can be valuable.

Women who have Become Pregnant During the Course of Maintenance Treatment

Management depends largely on when in the course of gestation pregnancy is recognized and on which medications are in use. As outlined above, patient preference is the key determinant in selecting treatment strategies. From the prospective of teratogenicity, the choice of rapid discontinuation becomes progressively less appealing as the pregnancy progresses beyond the first ten weeks. When this option is chosen, tapering over a one- to two-week period may reduce the risk of early relapse without substantially altering the risk of teratogenicity, but plans should be made in advance for intervention in the event of relapse, and close follow-up offered throughout.

Determine Appropriate Psychosocial Intervention

Specialized versions of psychosocial interventions such as family-focused therapy [37] interpersonal social rhythms therapy [38], life goals [39], and cognitive behavioral therapy [40] have shown promise as adjunctive interventions in the maintenance phase of treatment.

Even where these specific treatments are not readily available, it seems wise to incorporate the common elements of these good mood hygiene interventions into the treatment plan to whatever extent is feasible. The collaborative care model developed at Massachusetts General Hospital (MGH) recommends that patients use these elements to develop an individualized written management plan that does not rely entirely on the patient for executive function. Samples and directions for constructing treatment contracts can be accessed via the internet at www.manicdepressive.org.

Encourage Good Mood Hygiene

Treatment outcome can be improved in many cases by educating the patient and his or her family about the nature of the illness, encouraging self monitoring (such as keeping a simple daily mood chart), identifying potential triggers, and other principles of good mood hygiene. Although some studies associating environmental events with onset of episodes find little correlation beyond the earliest episodes, most patients are able to learn simple strategies to lessen conflict or avoid precipitants. Advising patients about the need to maintain stable sleep/wake, diet, and exercise schedules, the need to avoid extremes in work, and the need to take care when traveling across time zones is often beneficial. Although, like many of the somatic therapies described below, there are no empirical data showing their effectiveness in treatment refractory bipolar patients, the low cost and low risk associated with these strategies justifies their recommendation.

Since bipolar illness tends to be understood in biological terms, it is interesting that psychotherapy appears beneficial for bipolar patients. No verbal therapies claim acute antimanic benefits, but most forms of psychotherapy seem to augment the pro-phylactic benefit of lithium [41–46]. While the active elements of psychotherapy remain unclear, the prophylactic efficacy of verbal therapies, as with lithium treatment, appear to require continued treatment.

Among patients receiving lithium prophylaxis for at least three years, Priebe *et al.* found a significant association between relapse rates and negative expressed emotion by family members [47]. The impact of negative expressed emotion seems particularly strong in the early phase of an episode and during the period immediately following discharge from the hospital. Mood hygiene can be improved by helping family members deal constructively with the hostility aroused in relating to the bipolar patient. The impact of expressed emotion may play a role in psychotherapy as well. Numerous anecdotes suggest that during episodes of mania or severe depression insight-oriented therapies can have desta-bilizing effects on mood state. Therapists treating bipolar patients can improve mood hygiene by assessing mood state and making appropriate adjustments to the content, frequency, and duration of therapy sessions. As patients become acutely ill, it is most appropriate for sessions to become more frequent but briefer, with a focus on safety issues and control of acute symptoms. Many patients report beneficial experiences from self-help groups such as the Depression and Bipolar Support Alliance (DBSA).

Monitoring Visit Interval

There are no empirical data to guide the choice of interval between monitoring vis-its. Even within national boundaries, practice varies widely across geographic regions and treatment settings. The collaborative care model offers a flexible approach to monitoring intervals; the default recommendation is for monthly moni-toring visits throughout the remainder of one year following the end of the acute phase. Over the next year, patients remaining well are seen every other month. After two years in remission, patients are seen quarterly.

Maintain Prophylactic Treatments in Target Range

Although the boundaries of the therapeutic range for lithium (0.5–1.0 mmol/L), valproate (50–120 µg/ml), and carbamazepine (4–12 µg/ml) rest more on clinical tradition than empirical data, available data are generally consistent with the ideas that most patients will experience therapeutic benefit when above the lower bound and few will benefit only at levels about the upper bound. For clinical purposes, it is important to recognize that maintaining serum levels in the therapeutic range presents a broad and sometime shifting target at which clinical management aims. During the transition from the acute phase to the maintenance phase it is often necessary to adjust dosage of mood stabilizing medications. Tolerance of adverse effects generally decreases when acute manic symptoms resolve and, at least in the case of lithium and carbamazepine, serum levels change.

Manage Comorbid Conditions

It is unusual to find bipolar patients without comorbid conditions. Psychiatric comorbidity, especially common among bipolar patients, includes anxiety disorders, alcohol and substance abuse, as well as attention deficit and other disruptive behavior disorders of childhood. The national comorbidity study makes it clear that comorbidity is a significant risk factor predictive of relapse. Although representing only 14% of subjects with any diagnosis, the subset that met DSM criteria for three or more disorders accounted for 90% of the severe episodes that occurred over a year of follow-up [48].

Anxiety disorders are particularly common among bipolar patients seeking treatment. Simon *et al.* reported lifetime comorbid anxiety disorders occurred in over half of the first 500 subjects enrolled in the Systematic Treatment Enhancement Program for Bipolar Disorder (STEP-BD), and were associated with younger age of onset, decreased likelihood of recovery, poorer role functioning and quality of life, less time well, and greater likelihood of suicide attempts. Although substance abuse disorders were particularly prevalent among patients with anxiety disorders, anxiety comorbidity appeared to exert an independent, deleterious effect on functioning, frequently including a history of suicide attempts.

Untreated, these disorders contribute to dysphoria, counterproductive self-treatment, and, particularly when associated with insomnia, may interfere with treatment response. In many cases, treatment of these conditions has salutary effects on the course of bipolar illness or vice versa [49–51]. Unfortunately, standard treatment for some of these conditions (eg, treatment of obsessive compulsive disorder with selective serotonin reuptake inhibitors or amphetamine for attention deficit disorder) can exacerbate BD.

Use of an anxiolytic agent is often warranted to ameliorate symptoms of anxiety disorders, restore sleep, and truncate excessive response to stressors. Small open trials find high-potency benzodiazepines such as alprazolam and clonazepam often produce rapid benefit by significantly relieving dysphoria in some bipolar depressed patients [52,53]. It remains unclear, however, whether the patients described experienced a true antidepressant effect or simply improved scores on depression rating scales as a result of diminished anxiety.

For anxious patients with contraindication to benzodiazepines or nonresponse to benzodiazepine – gabapentin, topiramate, clonidine, or propranolol may be useful adjuncts. Adrenergic blockers must be used with caution since they may contribute to depression or interfere with antidepressant medications.

For bipolar patients who experience successful resolution of the acute-phase anxiety and maintain stability through the continuation phase, tapering of anxiolytic drugs is usually indicated. Some bipolar patients do, however, appear to benefit from maintenance anxiolytic therapy.

Bipolar patients appear to have a particular vulnerability to substance abuse, and substance abuse is associated with poor prognosis. Reports of dramatic increases in all-cause mortality and risk of suicide in untreated bipolar patients with substance abuse make it clear that treatment for substance abuse should be a priority in the treatment of bipolar illness [54,55].

Manage Adverse Effects

Nearly all bipolar patients will experience adverse effects attributable to maintenance treatment. A substantial proportion of otherwise treatment-responsive patients discontinue treatment due to adverse effects. At the MGH bipolar clinic the most common reasons for patients to discontinue successful treatment during the maintenance phase were weight gain, cognitive impairment, gastrointestinal complaints, and hair loss. Active management of adverse effects with patient education allows many patients to sustain beneficial treatment. This includes willingness to acknowledge the possibility that treatment is indeed causing the adverse effect and offering alternatives (*see* Table 5.4). Treatment discontinuation can often be avoided by changing the amount, timing, and form of problematic medications. This is particularly true for adverse effects such as nausea and tremor, which are associated with peak drug levels.

Roughening and Recurrence

Many patients experience intermittent subsyndromal symptoms (roughening) during the discontinuation/maintenance phase. The significance of roughening depends on whether it is understood as the harbinger of an impending acute episode or is merely a brief period of mild symptoms with little clear relation to the patient's mood disorder. Studies of such interepisode symptoms reported by Keller [56] and Fava [57] suggest that roughening with features of depression often resolves without intervention. Symptoms of hypomania carry a higher risk of evolving into full affective episodes.

The occurrence of symptoms meeting criteria for an acute episode are considered a recurrence (new episode) requiring reintroduction of acute treatments.

Endpoints

The main endpoints in the relapse prevention pathway involve interrupting the course of treatment aimed at relapse prevention when the patient suffers a new acute episode. Patients may enter the acute depression pathway or the mood elevation pathway for a course of acute treatment and re-enter the relapse prevention pathway after achieving a stable remission. Transitions to these pathways are common over the course of bipolar illness and need not be viewed as treatment failure. When treatment returns to the relapse prevention pathway, the question of altering the therapies aimed at relapse prevention should be addressed, based on whether the long-term trend indicates fewer, briefer, or milder episodes.

Treatment success, even when euthymia extends over a period of years, is not by itself an indication to discontinue treatment. Any decision to reduce treatments aimed at relapse prevention should be weighed in the context of potential risks and benefits.

References

1. Coryell W, Winokur G, Solomon D *et al.* **Lithium and recurrence in a long-term follow-up of bipolar affective disorder.** *Psychol Med* 1997; **27**:281–289.

2. Goodwin FK. **Anticonvulsant therapy and suicide risk in affective disorders.** *J Clin Psychiatry* 1999; **60**(Suppl 2):89–93; discussion 111–116.

3. Suppes T, Baldessarini RJ, Faedda GL *et al.* **Risk of recurrence following discontinuation of lithium treatment in bipolar disorder.** *Arch Gen Psychiatry* 1991; **48**:1082–1088.

4. Suppes T, Baldessarini RJ, Faedda GL *et al.* **Discontinuation of maintenance treatment in bipolar disorder: risks and implications.** *Harv Rev Psychiatry* 1993; **1**:131–144.

5. Faedda GL, Tondo L, Baldessarini RJ *et al.* **Outcome after rapid vs gradual discontinuation of lithium treatment in bipolar disorders.** *Arch Gen Psychiatry* 1993; **50**:448–455.

6. Bowden CL. **The ability of lithium and other mood stabilizers to decrease suicide risk and prevent relapse.** *Curr Psychiatry Rep* 2000; **2**:490–494.

7. Bowden CL. **Efficacy of lithium in mania and maintenance therapy of bipolar disorder.** *J Clin Psychiatry* 2000; **61**(Suppl 9):35–40.

8. Sachs GS, Printz DJ, Kahn DA *et al.* **The Expert Consensus Guideline Series: Medication Treatment of Bipolar Disorder 2000.** *Postgrad Med* 2000. Spec No:1–104.

9. Keck PE Jr, McElroy SL. **Outcome in the pharmacologic treatment of bipolar disorder.** *J Clin Psychopharmacol* 1996; **16**(Suppl 1):15S–23S.

10. Tohen M, Waternaux CM, Tsuang MT. **Outcome in mania. A 4-year prospective follow-up of 75 patients utilizing survival analysis.** *Arch Gen Psychiatry* 1990; **47**:1106–1111.

11. Tohen M, Strakowski SM, Zarate C Jr *et al.* **The McLean-Harvard first-episode project: 6-month symptomatic and functional outcome in affective and nonaffective psychosis.** *Biol Psychiatry* 2000; **48**:467–476.

12. Keller MB, Lavori PW, Coryell W *et al.* **Bipolar I: a five-year prospective follow-up.** *J Nerv Ment Dis* 1993; **181**:238–245.

13. Judd LL, Schettler PJ, Akiskal HS *et al.* **Long-term symptomatic status of bipolar I vs. bipolar II disorders.** *Int J Neuropsychopharmacol* 2003; **6**:127–137.

14. Maj M, Pirozzi R, Magliano L *et al.* **The prognostic significance of "switching" in patients with bipolar disorder: a 10-year prospective follow-up study.** *Am J Psychiatry* 2002; **159**:1711–1717.

15. Maj M, Pirozzi R, Starace F. **Previous pattern of course of the illness as a predictor of response to lithium prophylaxis in bipolar patients.** *J Affect Disord* 1989; **17**:237–241.

16. Maj M. **Clinical prediction of response to lithium prophylaxis in bipolar patients: the importance of the previous pattern of course of the illness.** *Clin Neuropharmacol* 1990; **13**(Suppl 1):S66–70.

17. Maj M, Veltro F, Pirozzi R *et al.* **Pattern of recurrence of illness after recovery from an episode of major depression: a prospective study.** *Am J Psychiatry* 1992; **149**:795–800.

18. Calabrese JR, Bowden CL, Sachs G *et al.* **A placebo-controlled 18-month trial of lamotrigine and lithium maintenance treatment in recently depressed patients with bipolar I disorder.** *J Clin Psychiatry* 2003; **64**:1013–1024.

19. Bowden CL, Calabrese JR, Sachs G *et al.* **A placebo-controlled 18-month trial of lamotrigine and lithium maintenance treatment in recently manic or hypomanic patients with bipolar I disorder.** *Arch Gen Psychiatry* 2003; **60**:392–400.

20. Tohen M, Ketter TA, Zarate CA *et al.* **Olanzapine versus divalproex sodium for the treatment of acute mania and maintenance of remission: a 47-week study.** *Am J Psychiatry* 2003; **160**:1263–1271.

21. Suppes T, Webb A, Paul B *et al.* **Clinical outcome in a randomized 1-year trial of clozapine versus treatment as usual for patients with treatment-resistant illness and a history of mania.** *Am J Psychiatry* 1999; **156**:1164–1169.

22. Silverstone T, Romans S. **Long term treatment of bipolar disorder.** *Drugs* 1996; **51**:367–382.

23. Russell JC, Rasmussen KG, O'Connor MK *et al.* **Long-term maintenance ECT: a retrospective review of efficacy and cognitive outcome.** *J Ect* 2003; **19**:4–9.

24. Altshuler L, Suppes T, Black D *et al.* **Impact of antidepressant discontinuation after acute bipolar depression remission on rates of depressive relapse at 1-year follow-up.** *Am J Psychiatry* 2003; **160**:1252–1262.

25. Frye MA, Ketter TA, Leverich GS *et al.* **The increasing use of polypharmacotherapy for refractory mood disorders: 22 years of study.** *J Clin Psychiatry* 2000; **61**:9–15.

26. Wehr TA, Goodwin FK. **Rapid cycling in manic-depressives induced by tricyclic antidepressants.** *Arch Gen Psychiatry* 1979; **36**:555–559.

27. Wehr T, Goodwin FK. **Tricyclics modulate frequency of mood cycles.** *Chronobiologia* 1979; **6**:377–385.

28. Altshuler LL, Post RM, Leverich GS *et al.* **Antidepressant-induced mania and cycle acceleration: a controversy revisited.** *Am J Psychiatry* 1995; **152**:1130–1138.

29. Kukopulos A, Reginaldi D, Laddomada P *et al.* **Course of the manic-depressive cycle and changes caused by treatment.** *Pharmakopsychiatr Neuropsychopharmakol* 1980; **13**:156–167.

30. Esparon J, Kolloori J, Naylor GJ *et al.* **Comparison of the prophylactic action of flupenthixol with placebo in lithium treated manic-depressive patients.** *Br J Psychiatry* 1986; **148**:723–725.

31. Dwight MM, Keck PE Jr, Stanton SP *et al.* **Antidepressant activity and mania associated with risperidone treatment of schizoaffective disorder.** *Lancet* 1994; **344**:554–555.

32. Simon AE, Aubry JM, Malky L *et al.* **Hypomania-like syndrome induced by olanzapine.** *Int Clin Psychopharmacol* 1999; **14**:377–378.

33. Prien RF, Himmelhoch JM, Kupfer DJ. Treatment of mixed mania. *J Affect Disord* 1988; **15**:9–15.

34. Schnur DB, Mukherjee S, Suckeim HA *et al.* Symptomatic predictors of ECT response in medication-nonresponsive manic patients. *J Clin Psychiatry* 1992; **53**:63–66.

35. Rabheru K, Persad E. A review of continuation and maintenance electroconvulsive therapy. *Can J Psychiatry* 1997; **42**:476–484.

36. Bonds C, Frye MA, Coudreaut MF *et al.* Cost reduction with maintenance ECT in refractory bipolar disorder. *J Ect* 1998; **14**:36–41.

37. Miklowitz DJ, Richards JA, George EL *et al.* Integrated family and individual therapy for bipolar disorder: results of a treatment development study. *J Clin Psychiatry* 2003; **64**:182–191.

38. Frank E, Novick D. Progress in the psychotherapy of mood disorders: studies from the Western Psychiatric Institute and Clinic. *Epidemiol Psichiatr Soc* 2001; **10**:245–252.

39. Bauer MS. An evidence-based review of psychosocial treatments for bipolar disorder. *Psychopharmacol Bull* 2001; **35**:109–134.

40. Otto MW, Reilly-Harrington N, Sachs GS. Psychoeducational and cognitive-behavioral strategies in the management of bipolar disorder. *J Affect Disord* 2003; **73**:171–181.

41. Mayo JA. Marital therapy with manic-depressive patients treated with lithium. *Compr Psychiatry* 1979; **20**:419–426.

42. Lesser IM, Godofsky ID. Group treatment for chronic patients: educational and supervisory aspects. *Int J Group Psychother* 1983; **33**:535–546.

43. Vasile RG, Samson JA, Bemporad J *et al.* A biopsychosocial approach to treating patients with affective disorders. *Am J Psychiatry* 1987; **144**:341–344.

44. Miklowitz DJ, Goldstein MJ, Nuechterlein KH *et al.* Family factors and the course of bipolar affective disorder. *Arch Gen Psychiatry* 1988; **45**:225–231.

45. Van Gent EM, Via SL, Zwart FM. Group therapy in addition to lithium therapy in patients with bipolar disorder. *Acta Psychiatr Belg* 1988; **88**:405–418.

46. Kanas N. Group psychotherapy with bipolar patients: a review and synthesis. *Int J Group Psychother* 1993; **43**:321–333.

47. Priebe S, Wildgrube C, Muller-Oerlinghausen B *et al.* Lithium prophylaxis and expressed emotion. *Br J Psychiatry* 1989; **154**:396–399.

48. Kessler RC, Stang P, Wittchen HU *et al.* Lifetime co-morbidities between social phobia and mood disorders in the US National Comorbidity Survey. *Psychol Med* 1999; **29**:555–67.

49. Winokur G, Coryell W, Endicott J *et al.* Familial alcoholism in manic-depressive (bipolar) disease. *Am J Med Genet* 1996; **67**:197–201.

50. Brady KT. Difficulties in diagnosis and management of bipolar disorder: three case presentations. *J Clin Psychiatry* 2000; **61**(suppl 13):32–37.

51. Brady KT, Lydiard RB. Bipolar affective disorder and substance abuse. *J Clin Psychopharmacol* 1992; **12**(Suppl 1):17S–22S.

52. Kishimoto A, Kamata K, Sugihara T *et al.* Treatment of depression with clonazepam. *Acta Psychiatr Scand* 1988; **77**:81–86.

53. Rush AJ, Schlesser MA, Erman M *et al.* Alprazolam in bipolar-I depressions. *Pharmacotherapy* 1984; **4**: 40–42.

54. Nilsson A. Mortality in recurrent mood disorders during periods on and off lithium. A complete population study in 362 patients. *Pharmacopsychiatry* 1995; **28**:8–13.

55. Nilsson A. Lithium therapy and suicide risk. *J Clin Psychiatry* 1999; **60**(Suppl):2.

56. Keller MB, Lavori PW, Kane JM *et al.* Subsyndromal symptoms in bipolar disorder. A comparison of standard and low serum levels of lithium. *Arch Gen Psychiatry* 1992; **49**:371–376.

57. Fava GA, Kellner R. Prodromal symptoms in affective disorders. *Am J Psychiatry* 1991; **48**:823–830.

Chapter 6

Rapid Cycling Pathway

Introduction

Rapid cycling, defined by the occurrence of four or more episodes or two complete cycles (two high and two low phases in a 12-month period), is a term coined by Dunner and Feive to describe a common finding among bipolar patients they considered to have a poor response to lithium [1,2].

Clinicians searching for evidence-based guidance should be aware that it is easy to misinterpret study data pertaining to rapid cycling. Careful review of methods sections is often necessary to determine whether the outcomes reported pertain to rapid cycling *per se*, or, as is more often the case, represent other outcomes for bipolar subjects with a prior history of rapid cycling, or bipolar subjects who met criteria for rapid cycling in the preceding year.

The prevalence of rapid cycling is estimated to be 5–15% of those with bipolar disorder (BD), but many recent studies report much higher rates. The National Institute of Mental Health (NIMH) collaborative study reports that of 345 bipolar subjects followed over an average of 13 years of follow-up, 25.8% experienced at least one year meeting criteria for rapid cycling [3].

Most studies find a female gender predominance among rapid cycling. Reported female:male gender ratios ranging from 2:1–9:1 can be misleading since these ratios also reflect the presence of more women than men in treatment-seeking populations [4]. Despite some inconsistency between studies, hypothyroidism is considered a strong risk factor for rapid cycling.

Studies of cycle frequency find that its distribution is skewed toward higher frequency cycling. It can be difficult to evaluate patients with brief cycle lengths. There is no reliable way to differentiate ultrarapid cycling (cycle length <24–48 hours) from mixed episodes, nor is there clinical reason to approach the treatment of these conditions differently.

The fourth edition of the Diagnostic and Statistical Manual (DSM-IV) designates rapid cycling as a course specifier rather than as a distinct subtype of bipolar illness. The vast majority of bipolar patients who experience a period of rapid cycling during the course of their illness will also experience periods without rapid cycling. Even when not meeting the criteria for rapid cycling *per se*, patients with a history of rapid cycling tend to have more episodes, shorter well intervals, and a higher rate of suicide attempts than patients who have never had rapid cycling [4,5]. These findings suggest a history of rapid cycling could be regarded as a clinical trait marker indicating poor prognosis.

Persistence of rapid cycling over periods of years appears to be the exception rather than the rule. Patients with sustained rapid cycling should be carefully evaluated for possible substance abuse and other medical conditions which might account for the pattern of sustained rapid cycling (medications, sleep apnea, multiple sclerosis, head injury, mental retardation, electroencephalogram [EEG] abnormalities).

Evidence from Statistically Valid Studies

Available category A evidence for rapid cycling consists of only one double-blind placebo-controlled parallel group study, which found lamotrigine superior to placebo over six months of follow-up [6]. The overall advantage for lamotrigine was due largely to the robust benefit in rapid cycling bipolar II subjects. Therefore, lamotrigine is the only evidence-based first-line treatment for bipolar II rapid cycling.

In the absence of category A or even category B evidence supporting any agent for rapid cycling bipolar I patients, equipoise options must be drawn from the literature more broadly. Several small category C studies with mirror design suggest lithium is in fact beneficial for control of rapid cycling. Four studies suggest patients with an Mania, Depression, Interval (MDI) symptom free episode pattern, in which subjects cycle directly from mania to depression, derive a greater anticycling benefit from lithium than those with other episode patterns [7–10]. Case series [11] and single reports suggest lamotrigine and agents beneficial for acute mania may reduce cycling in bipolar I patients. Literature suggesting that, compared with lithium, patients with rapid cycling respond better to valproate, carbamazepine, and dopamine-blocking agents, is mainly confined to reports of outcomes for single episodes of mania [12,13]. These treatments with known efficacy should be offered before attempts are made to manage this potentially dangerous condition with unproven alternatives.

Initiating Treatment

Treatment for rapid cycling is, by definition, aimed at reducing cycle frequency, and might be considered as a special instance of relapse prevention. While true in the abstract, the clinical reality is somewhat paradoxical. Patients with rapid cycling typically present with varying degrees of acute symptomatology and fluctuating polarity. Treatment of rapid cycling and nonrapid cycling patients differs most in the management of acute-phase symptomatology rather than in the continuation or maintenance-phase management. Because rapid cycling is a course specifier, and the outcome of clinical interest is a change in longitudinal course, there is no urgent care approach appropriate for rapid cycling.

Anticycling interventions are organized sequentially and adequate time should be allotted to evaluate the results.

Patients enter the rapid cycling pathway if their current clinical status is compatible with avoiding or tapering standard antidepressants or other cycle-promoting agents. The first step in treatment directed against cycling should be to establish a mood-stabilizing regime which eliminates cycle-promoting agents and adds or optimizes medications with mood-stabilizing properties. In practice this most often means tapering off antidepressant medications, steroids, sympathomimetics, and stimulants (including caffeine) (*see* Table 5.3). Consideration should be given to eliminating any other agents that have been implicated as cycle-promoting or inducing mania (dehydroepiandrosterone [DHEA], bronchodilators, gonadotropins, oral contraceptives, muscle relaxants, triazolobenzodiazepines).

Reports from Kukopolos and Wehr suggest that iatrogenic factors frequently fuel rapid cycling [10,14]. Therefore, although not a designation in the DSM, it can be useful to classify rapid cycling as primary or secondary.

Considerations for Special Subpopulations

Primary Rapid Cycling

Primary rapid cycling describes persistent recurrence over at least four months in the absence of antidepressant medications, or other substances, or a general medical condition that is associated with induction of mania or promoting cycling. Primary rapid cycling is frequently difficult to treat and can be made worse by cycle-promoting agents.

Secondary Rapid Cycling

Secondary rapid cycling refers to instances where a secondary factor is believed to play an etiological role in sustaining a rate of cycling that would otherwise be less than four per year. In most such cases, the BD is correctly diagnosed as a primary mood disorder, but the pattern of rapid cycling is secondary (substance induced or due to a general medical condition). Secondary rapid cycling is often responsive to elimination or amelioration of factors which might destabilize mood or promote cycling. Some bipolar patients with apparent secondary rapid cycling become intensely dysphoric or even euphoric soon after tapering standard antidepressant medication. These patients can be managed by shifting to acute-phase management, and after achieving remission again, resuming taper on a more gradual schedule.

80

Treat Comorbid Condition as a Putative Cause of Secondary Rapid Cycling

Comorbid conditions should be treated as putative causes of secondary rapid cycling, particularly for patients with comorbid conditions such as obsessive-compulsive disorder (OCD), panic, bulimia, attention-deficit hyperactivity disorder (ADHD) or migraine. Where the preferred treatments for a comorbid condition may fuel rapid cycling, the preferable option is to attempt to treat the comorbid condition by maximizing or adding a mood stabilizer. Several medications classified as putative mood stabilizers have been shown to have salutary effects on one or more common comorbid conditions. When this proves unsuccessful, alternative treatment for the comorbid condition without cycle-promoting properties should be attempted (eg, clonidine for ADHD). If a third intervention is required (eg, severe comorbid OCD responsive only to selective serotonin reuptake inhibitors [SSRIs]), minimizing the dose of the offending agent to a level just sufficient to allow treatment with cognitive behavioral therapy offers a compromise between conflicting treatment objectives.

Common Decision Points

A summary of common decision points in the rapid cycling pathway is shown in Table 6.1.

Common Decision Points		
	Decision Points	Suggested Starting Point
1	Determine need for acute-phase antidepressant treatment	Review current symptom acuity and cycle frequency over past 4 episodes
2	Identify possible secondary factors	*See* Table 5.3
3	Taper any antidepressants	20–33% per month
4	Optimize/add anticycling agents	Lamotrigine, lithium, or valproate if not already present
5	Evaluate outcome	Use systematic assessment and prospective charting
6	Add additional anticycling agent(s)	See menu of putative mood-stabilizing agents
7	When to shift priority to management of acute episode	Evaluate safety and patient tolerance

Table 6.1

Determine Appropriate Acute-Phase Treatment

Treatment for acute mania generally does not conflict with treatment for rapid cycling. Occasional case reports which have implicated phenothiazines as cycle-promoting agents in individual cases make avoiding these agents worthy of consideration.

Treatment for depression is much more problematic. As a rule the deciding factor in prescribing antidepressants to rapid cycling patients is the patient's ability to tolerate and safely endure periods of dysphoria. At any time patient–doctor judgment deems it appropriate, the care of rapid cycling patients can be shifted to the approach usual for acute bipolar depression and standard antidepressant medications can be administered judiciously. There are, however, circumstances in which the use of antidepressants can be discouraged as imprudent. For instance, standard antidepressant medications are unlikely to benefit patients with a history of dysphoria lasting less than two weeks, or those for whom prior treatment trials demonstrate a duration of remission shorter than four weeks, despite continued treatment with standard antidepressants.

In the many instances in which patients are willing to abstain from standard antidepressants, the primary objectives of acute treatment become maintaining safety while implementing interventions that can relieve the dysphoria without adversely affecting the course of illness. Such interventions are, by definition, mood stabilizers, and may include lithium, anticonvulsants, atypical antipsychotics, and cholinesterase inhibitors (donepezil), as well as psychosocial interventions.

Optimize/Add Anticycling Agents

Selection of Mood Stabilizer

There are few controlled prospective studies of rapid cycling. Patients with rapid cycling respond less well to lithium than nonrapid cycling patients. To generalize from this observation that lithium is not beneficial for rapid cycling is, however, misleading. Clear-cut nonresponse to lithium is observed only when response is defined narrowly as having no recurrences at all. Available literature does, however, indicate a consistent benefit of lithium in reducing cycle frequency [7,15–17].

Given the refractory nature of rapid cycling, all putative mood-stabilizing medications and antimanic agents may be considered rational options for treatment of rapid cycling, but preference should be given to agents with established mood-stabilizing or antimanic efficacy.

Although there are no prospective comparative data, uncontrolled reports of good treatment response to anticonvulsant medications such as valproate or carbamazepine in patients with a history of rapid cycling and nonresponse to lithium have established these agents as preferable to lithium as initial treatment for rapid cycling. As illustrated in Figure 6.1, the recommended pathway starts with two interventions, tapering any antidepressants and adding either lamotrigine, divalproex, or lithium.

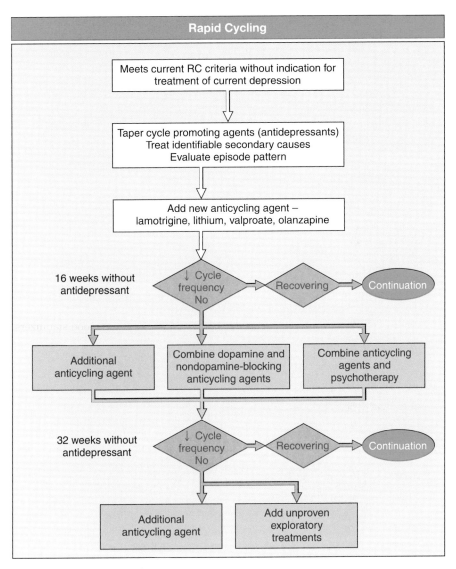

Figure 6.1. RC, rapid cycling.

Several reports indicate that some patients refractory to a first-line anticycling agent may respond well to a wide array of treatments, including atypical antipsychotic medications (clozapine, risperidone, olanzapine, quetiapine), other anticonvulsants (lamotrigine, gabapentin, topiramate), thyroxine, calcium-channel blockers, cholinomimetics (donepezil, choline), omega-3 fatty acids, bright light, and electroconvulsive therapy

(ECT). Unfortunately, these reports often draw optimistic conclusions based on the presumptive benefit of an intervention on the outcome of a single episode.

Psychosocial interventions may be beneficial in ameliorating depression and reducing recurrence of depression. Several promising psychosocial interventions developed specifically for bipolar illness target reducing interpersonal conflict, management of potential episode triggers, and/or stabilizing circadian rhythms.

Evaluating Outcome

The inferential error of *post hoc, ergo propter hoc*, is particularly difficult to avoid in managing rapid cycling patients. In evaluating the impact of each anticycling intervention, mere resolution of a current acute episode should not be considered evidence of improvement in itself nor should any single recurrence be taken as treatment failure. Prospective mood charts can help guide treatment decision making, especially if they provide clear evidence of fewer, briefer, or milder episodes. Even in the face of intermittent periods of severe depression and/or mania, evidence of decreased cycle frequency over the first three months of taper is often the harbinger of progressive improvement. The benefit of adding a new mood stabilizer or discontinuing antidepressants may not be apparent for several months. Thus, in assessing outcome of interventions in this pathway, little confidence can be given to presumed effects observed over time periods less than three cycle lengths or four months. For most interventions, evidence of efficacy often requires sustained treatment over six months or longer.

Add Additional Anticycling Agent(s)

Clinical imperatives make it unreasonable to delay adding new interventions for periods longer than four months. Titration of each intervention to an individual's optimal dose is an art greatly aided by thoughtful review of a daily mood chart (*see* Appendix 2). Upward titration to maximal dose of each mood stabilizer is a reasonable option limited by the tolerability of each agent. After three cycle lengths or six months at a given dose, agents with no apparent benefit may be tapered off. Patients with partial benefit may be given additional time on the current regime or additional agents can be added.

Patients remain in the rapid cycling pathway until treatment achieves a stable remission which, in theory, would allow management of acute depressive episodes in the same manner as nonrapid cycling patients. Logically, this judgment implies rapid cycling has been broken, but there are no data to determine if, in fact, absence of the rapid cycling state indicates a transition to a less pernicious disease state, or simple lack of overt expression of an enduring trait. With this caution, suggested minimal criteria for exiting the rapid cycling pathway when well require a stable recovery for at least one year.

Consequently, the long-term management of the majority of rapid cycling patients remains in the rapid cycling pathway even though their rate of recurrence no longer meets the criteria for rapid cycling. The major focus for patients experiencing one to three episodes per year is to use the iterative treatment/assessment process to progressively improve their overall regime aiming at the highest possible quality of life. Records documenting incremental improvement over the span of years are invaluable assets for maintaining the therapeutic optimism of patient, family and clinician as well as guiding the next therapeutic trial.

Endpoints

The main endpoints in the rapid cycling pathway involve either interrupting the course of treatment aimed at rapid cycling in order to treat intolerable acute symptoms or declaring the patient recovered from rapid cycling.

When the patient suffers an acute episode which requires treatment with standard antidepressant medications, therapeutic focus shifts from rapid cycling to standard management of acute bipolar depression. Patients may also require management in accordance with the acute mania pathway. Transitions to these pathways are common over the course of bipolar illness. When the acute symptoms remit, treatment returns to the rapid cycling pathway.

Patients meeting remission criteria for more than one year are candidates for transition to the standard relapse prevention pathway. Clinicians and patients should be aware that leaving the rapid cycling pathway – and its more restrictive guidelines – carries with it an as yet unsubstantiated assumption that rapid cycling represents a state rather than a trait. When selecting treatment for the next new episode, even a distant history of rapid cycling should be taken into account.

References

1. Dunner DL, Patrick V, Fieve RR. **Rapid cycling manic depressive patients.** *Compr Psychiatry* 1977; **18**:561–566.

2. Dunner DL, Fleiss JL, Fieve RR. **Lithium carbonate prophylaxis failure.** *Br J Psychiatry* 1976; **129**:40–44.

3. Coryell W, Endicott J, Keller M. **Rapidly cycling affective disorder. Demographics, diagnosis, family history, and course.** *Arch Gen Psychiatry* 1992; **49**:126–131.

4. Baldessarini RJ, Tondo L, Floris G *et al.* **Effects of rapid cycling on response to lithium maintenance treatment in 360 bipolar I and II disorder patients.** *J Affect Disord* 2000; **61**:13–22.

5. Coryell W, Solomon D, Turvey C *et al.* **The long-term course of rapid-cycling bipolar disorder.** *Arch Gen Psychiatry* 2003; **60**:914–920.

6. Calabrese JR, Suppes T, Bowden CL *et al.* **A double-blind, placebo-controlled, prophylaxis study of lamotrigine in rapid-cycling bipolar disorder. Lamictal 614 Study Group.** *J Clin Psychiatry* 2000; **61**:841–850.

7. Maj M. **Clinical prediction of response to lithium prophylaxis in bipolar patients: the importance of the previous pattern of course of the illness.** *Clin Neuropharmacol* 1990; **13**(Suppl 1):S66–70.

8. Grof E, Haag M, Grof P *et al.* **Lithium response and the sequence of episode polarities: preliminary report on a Hamilton sample.** *Prog Neuropsychopharmacol Biol Psychiatry* 1987; **11**:199–203.

9. Haag H, Heidorn A, Haag M *et al.* **Sequence of affective polarity and lithium response: preliminary report on Munich sample.** *Prog Neuropsychopharmacol Biol Psychiatry* 1987; **11**:205–208.

10. Kukopulos A, Reginaldi D, Laddomada P *et al.* **Course of the manic-depressive cycle and changes caused by treatment.** *Pharmakopsychiatr Neuropsychopharmakol* 1980; **13**:156–167.

11. Bowden CL, Calabrese JR, McElroy SL *et al.* **The efficacy of lamotrigine in rapid cycling and non-rapid cycling patients with bipolar disorder.** *Biol Psychiatry* 1999; **45**:953–958.

12. Swann AC, Bowden CL, Calabrese JR *et al.* **Pattern of response to divalproex, lithium, or placebo in four naturalistic subtypes of mania.** *Neuropsychopharmacology* 2002; **26**:530–536.

13. Gonzalez-Pinto A, Tohen M, Lalaguna B *et al.* **Treatment of bipolar I rapid cycling patients during dysphoric mania with olanzapine.** *J Clin Psychopharmacol* 2002; **22**:450–454.

14. Wehr TA, Goodwin FK. **Rapid cycling in manic-depressives induced by tricyclic antidepressants.** *Arch Gen Psychiatry* 1979; **36**:555–559.

15. Maj M. **The effect of lithium in bipolar disorder: a review of recent research evidence.** *Bipolar Disord* 2003; **5**:180–188.

16. Tondo L, Hennen J, Baldessarini RJ. **Rapid-cycling bipolar disorder: effects of long-term treatments.** *Acta Psychiatr Scand* 2003; **108**:4–14.

17. Koukopoulos A, Sani G, Koukopoulos AE *et al.* **Duration and stability of the rapid-cycling course: a long-term personal follow-up of 109 patients.** *J Affect Disord* 2003; **73**:75–85.

Chapter 7

Suicide Prevention

Introduction

Unlike the other pathways, which have entry and exit points and little overlap, suicide prevention is integral to the overall program of disease management for bipolar disorder (BD) and is an important treatment objective. Suicide is the eighth leading cause of death in the United States – each year approximately 30,000 people die in this way – and for every completed suicide, there are an estimated 25 attempts [1]. According to the Centers for Disease Control, almost all people who kill themselves have a diagnosable mental or substance abuse disorder, or both [2,3]. Therefore, early recognition and treatment of depression and substance abuse, or other acute psychiatric illness, may offer a promising means of preventing suicide and suicidal behavior.

Data indicating a high risk for suicide among patients with BD in particular makes a compelling case for emphasizing recognition and intervention in this potentially deadly illness. Approximately 48% of patients with BD make at least one suicide attempt [4]. The majority of suicides among patients with BD occur in association with the depressed phase [5,6] and most are carried out within the first few years of onset of the illness [7–9]. Although the high rates of suicidal behavior (defined as suicide, suicide attempt, or suicidal ideation) associated with BD may be greatly reduced by treatment [10–13], the clinical need for assessment and management of suicide risk remains constant.

The approach outlined here is adapted from a Systematic Treatment Enhancement Program for Bipolar Disorder (STEP-BD) work group that conducted a series of meetings and drafted general recommendations to help clinicians manage the risk of suicide for bipolar patients [14]. The simple approach offered below is far from comprehensive and is not intended as a clinical or legal standard. It aims, however, to encourage ongoing monitoring and provides a range of practical responses applicable to managing the risk of suicide in bipolar patients over a wide range of common critical clinical decision points.

Integration of Suicide Prevention into a Multiphase Treatment Strategy

In the absence of means to predict suicide accurately, clinicians must manage the risk by systematic assessment and by establishing suicide prevention as a priority objective on the collaborative care treatment plan. This chapter begins by considering the opportunities for integrating suicide prevention strategies into the general approach to treatment (as described in Chapter 1), with a focus on the initiation of a treatment relationship and on the issues arising during ongoing management in the acute, continuation, and maintenance phases of treatment. More specific recommendations are then offered for assessment and interventions.

Initiation of Treatment

Soon after a bipolar patient enters therapy, psychiatrists often find favorable opportunities to educate patients about their illness, treatment options, and good mood hygiene strategies. The discussion of bipolar illness should include suicidality as a potential and therefore expectable symptom of the disease and an issue to be addressed when establishing a management plan. An initial individualized plan can be based on a review of current and lifetime risk factors (*see* Table 7.1) and may draw on interventions such as those offered in Table 7.2.

Assess Inclination and Opportunity as Component Factors of Current Risk

The treating clinician's review of known current risk factors, organized in terms of inclination and opportunity as outlined in Table 7.2, should include (but is not limited to) assessment of stressors, level of agitation, current mood state, and substance abuse, as well as suicidal ideation. In addition, lifetime risk factors such as presence or absence of prior attempts should be discussed.

Time pressures frequently impede the clinician's ability to consistently capitalize on this opportunity. Even when time allows for discussion, memory decay over time often blunts the impact of verbal interventions. Further erosion occurs when the burden of relaying the information and treatment plan to family members and other care providers is taken on by a symptomatic patient. This often leaves the patient without a clear plan or supports at times of greatest need. The simple practical measures described below can help overcome these barriers to assessment.

Use Enduring Materials to Improve Educational Communications

A written care plan that anticipates as many contingencies as possible can reduce communication problems and sometimes prevent negative outcomes. Routine distribution of enduring instructional materials can increase the frequency, volume, and consistency of information communicated by the treating psychiatrist in regard to suicidality. To achieve this end while minimizing time demands on the treating psychiatrist, STEP-BD provides an informational videotape and written materials in the form of a Collaborative Care Workbook [24]. The workbook is designed to both transmit essential information and enable the patient to establish a written treatment plan. Other suitable enduring materials are available from patient advocacy groups and professional societies and can be used as means to provide information about suicidal behavior [25]. These resources are summarized in Table 7.3.

Suicide Risk Factors	
Factors Related to Inclination	
Risk Factor	**Comment**
Current episode	Suicidal behavior is most associated with current depressive and mixed episodes [12]
Course	Mania depression euthymia biphasic episode pattern, rapid cycling
Alcohol, substance abuse and other comorbid conditions	Untreated alcohol or psychoactive substance abuse greatly increases the risk of suicide [10]. Other comorbid conditions such as panic disorder, post-traumatic stress disorder, and ADHD are also associated with increased risk and warrant treatment [15]
Gender	Completed suicide ratio 4:1 male:female Suicide attempt ratio: 1:3 male:female
History of prior (aggressive/ impulsive) attempts	A history of prior suicide attempts characterizes the bipolar subpopulation at the highest risk for suicidal behavior. For this subpopulation the collaborative care plan serves as a means of increasing the awareness of all those involved in the patient's care of signs and symptoms associated with past high-risk situations. At the outset of treatment, individuals who have expressed suicidal behavior previously are encouraged to establish a specific antisuicide component in their own plans aimed at minimizing inclination and opportunity for self-harm. Patients with a history of impulsive self-destructive behavior present a problem for monitoring, since the presence of suicidal ideation is not a reliable indicator of immediate risk. Identification of individual triggers and coping strategies which emphasize reduction of opportunity may benefit some patients. Use of lithium or other medications with impact on impulsivity may also be helpful
Family history of suicide/suicide attempts	This was found to double the risk of suicide compared to the general population and operates independently of the risk of affective illness [16,17]
Race/ethnicity	Caucasians at higher risk [18,19]
Age	Adolescents and the elderly are high-risk groups [20–22]
Marital status	Higher risk in non-married individuals especially those with no dependents [23]
First year post-diagnosis	Bipolar patients within their first year of diagnosis constitute a group with a special need for education about the potential risk for suicide. Clinical research demonstrates heightened risk in the first year post-diagnosis [13]. Thus, establishing a written collaborative care plan between patient, support network, and clinician is recommended even for first-episode patients without prior suicidal behavior. Recognition of periods of heightened risk such as recurrence of acute affective illness and early intervention are two prevention strategies that may reduce the risk of suicide. A collaborative care plan can inform and empower supports designated by the patient to be involved in the prevention of suicide

Table 7.1. ADHD, attention deficit hyperactivity disorder.

Suicide Risk Factors	
Factors Related to Opportunity	
Risk Factor	**Comment**
Easy access to firearms (or identifiable lethal equivalent)	Patients in possession of firearms or other lethal equivalents maintain a high opportunity for suicide. The close proximity of access to lethal means creates a high-risk situation in a disorder with a risk of suicide that is, on its own, significant. Action is recommended to reduce access to firearms or other lethal means
Social isolation	Suicide rates are generally highest in areas of low population density and among those with few social supports [16]
Not in treatment	Treatment contract can help maintain therapeutic involvement and can include specific suicide risk management plan. Support networks are recommended to minimize the amount of time a patient spends in isolation and to limit access to lethal means thereby limiting a patient's opportunity

Table 7.1. *(continued)*

Discussion of suicide risk with new patients takes place with the aim of including risk reduction strategies in the patient's written treatment plan. The plan can then be distributed to supports designated by the patient. The inclusion of other supports empowered by the patient is an important feature of the plan. Such supports make it possible to avoid the obvious limitations of plans which rely solely on the patient's judgment to recognize danger and formulate an action plan. Thus, under optimal conditions, the patient and their supports have considered the issue of suicide risk and have an existing care plan that includes an individualized suicide risk management plan. This plan can be activated whenever necessary. Under less optimal circumstances, the recommendations provided below can be modified for immediate use by patients without a prior collaborative care plan. Using the template provided in Appendix 5, an initial "default plan" can often be formulated in a matter of minutes. Since the clinician may determine the need for specific interventions at the first visit, the rapidity and efficiency derived from the availability of a template can enhance the safety of options less restrictive than involuntary hospitalization.

Multiphase Treatment Strategy

Suicide prevention strategies can be integrated into the multiphase treatment strategy used across all phases of bipolar illness (for a more complete description of these concepts *see* Chapter 1). Prioritizing patient needs separately during the acute, continuation, and maintenance phases of treatment adds clarity to the complex task of treatment planning (*see* Table 7.4).

Interventions

Nonspecific Interventions

To Reduce Inclination
Sustain therapeutic relationships
Sustain periods of wellness
Abstain from alcohol and unprescribed use of mood-altering substances
Treat substance abuse
Create a treatment contract with doctors and significant others, to empower them in high-risk situations
Keep a daily mood chart
Develop a list of triggers to depressive episodes
List 25 pleasurable activities and choose at least one each day
Maintain contact with treating doctors
Assess suicidal ideation at each clinical visit
Allow time for recovery before returning to work or school
Tell people ahead of time not to take offense to provocative statements
Ask supports not to ask you to do things that will be more of a burden on you
Plan future-oriented activities

To Minimize Opportunity
Restrict access to firearms
Minimize access to lethal means
Educate significant others to risk of suicide
Encourage social contact

Specific Interventions

To Reduce Inclination

Treat acute episodes (specifically depression)	Sustain periods of wellness
Minimize time spent in isolation	Increase social contacts
Assess suicidal ideation at each clinical visit	Activate treatment contract
Maintain adherence to medication treatment	Attend AA/NA meetings
Keep patient's home alcohol and drug free	Participate in religious affiliation
Maintain good sleep hygiene and regular schedule	Maintain good personal hygiene
Consider psychotherapy	Learn a thought-stopping technique
Keep a journal	Limit caffeine intake
Implement problem solving and coping skills	Exercise

To Minimize Opportunity
Remove firearms, toxins, drugs
Eliminate stockpile of potential toxins (drugs)
Educate significant others to current risk of suicide
Encourage social contact
Minimize time spent in isolation
Include a contingency plan for responding to missed appointments
Include a contingency plan to manage decisions to end therapeutic relationships
Consider hospitalization

Table 7.2. AA, Alcoholics Anonymous; NA, Narcotics Anonymous.

Resources for Suicide Prevention Strategies		
Organization	**Telephone Number**	**Website**
National Suicide Hotline	1-800-SUICIDE (1-800-784-2433)	www.suicidehotlines.com
SAVE (Suicide Awareness, Voices of Education)		www.save.org
AFSP (American Foundation for Suicide Prevention)		www.afsp.org
Covenant House	1-800-999-9999	Link from www.afsp.org
Suicide and Suicide Prevention		www.psycom.net/depression.central.suicide.html
National Mental Health Association	1-800-433-5959	www.nmha.org
AAS (American Association of Suicidology)	(202) 237-2280	www.suicidology.org/understandingsuicide.htm

Table 7.3.

Acute-Phase Issues

During the acute phase of treatment, the priorities are safety and amelioration of acute symptoms that frequently include suicidality. The task of sustaining therapeutic optimism in the face of nihilism can be made easier when shared by a team of well-informed supports armed with a long list of potential interventions (*see* Table 7.2). Patient and care providers alike often derive strength from the knowledge that many options remain available, and by realistic understanding of the expected time lag required before antidepressant and other psychotropic interventions become effective.

Continuation-Phase Issues

Although the transition from acute depression to continuation-phase treatment is easily made as the patient becomes minimally symptomatic, the transition from continuation phase to maintenance phase is more problematic because recovering to recovered status seldom occurs smoothly. The early phase of improvement can potentially heighten the risk of suicide by restoring energy and motivation to an otherwise suicidally-depressed patient. Such apparent improvement may free the patient to act on morbid impulses or return them prematurely to the scrutiny of school or work, thereby exposing the patient to additional demoralizing stressors.

Integration of Suicide Prevention Strategies into Multiphase Treatment Plan		
Phase	**General**	**Suicide Prevention**

New patient intake	1. Education to understand bipolar illness and treatment options
	2. Determine diagnosis
	  a. Current clinical status
	  b. Lifetime diagnosis
	  c. Comorbid conditions
	3. Implement initial treatment plan
	4. Develop collaborative care plan
	5. Encourage support building
		1. Discuss bipolar illness as a suicide risk factor and need to manage risk
		2. Assess other risk and protective factors
		3. Include suicide prevention module in collaborative care plan
		4. Determine need to immediate specific intervention

All follow-up visits	1. Determine current clinical status
	2. Monitor
	  - Stressors
	  - Comorbid conditions
	  - Psychoactive substance use
	  - Treatment response
	  - Adverse effects
	  - Adherence/concordance
	3. Determine follow-up interval
		1. Assess potential suicidality. Monitor inclination and opportunity
		2. Determine need to immediate specific intervention. (*see* Table 7.5 for decision points and management suggestions)

Acute episode	1. Treatment for depression/mania
	2. Implement harm reduction strategies as per collaborative care plan
		1. Assure safety
		  a. Review current personal risk factors
		  b. Review/activate personal protective factors
		  c. Choose venue adequate for management of current inclination and opportunity
		  d. Dispense medications in safe quantity
		  e. Determine need to alert supports
		  f. Determine follow-up interval

Continuation phase	Continue acute treatment strategies	1. Continue acute treatment strategies 2. Monitor inclination and opportunity

Maintenance phase	1. Revise collaborative care plan
	2. Implement prophylactic strategies
	  a. Monitor for impending episodes
	  b. Manage adverse effects
		1. Consider revision of suicide prevention strategies
		  a. Pharmacological
		  b. Support building
		  c. Formal psychotherapies

Table 7.4

For many patients, despite sustained acute-phase treatment, the early months of recovery include weeks in which the full symptomatology of acute depression returns transiently. Such subsyndromal "relapses" are to be expected and indicate a

Basic Clinical Decision Points at Follow-Up	
Initial Decision Points	**Suggested Starting Point**
1 Assess current requirement for specific management of acute suicidality versus non-specific management	If active suicidal ideation, determine if acceptable supports are available for outpatient management
2 Discuss risk of suicide attempt and need to manage risk	Enhance communication with enduring materials: direct to collaborative care workbook, general patient/family information
3 Review current personal risk factors	Review suicide risk factors: inclination, opportunity, supports
4 Review current personal protective factors	Review of suicide protective factors: inclination, opportunity, supports
5 Determine need for immediate specific intervention	Treatment to alter inclination/reduce opportunity: increase support/limit isolation
6 Encourage incorporation of specific harm reduction strategy	Create or revise collaborative care plan
7 Determine appropriate follow-up interval	Schedule follow-up if confident interval is safe or hospitalize
8 Determined quantity of medication to be dispensed	Review potential for overdose, and alternatives for dispensing medication

Table 7.5

need for maintaining vigilance regarding the risk for suicide and the need to minimize opportunities for self-harm.

Maintenance-Phase Issues

When the indicators of inclination diminish, risk reduction strategies can be gradually tapered. Patients frequently experience the resolution of suicidal ideation upon recovery from the acute episode and express desire to reduce the level of suicide precautions. Care providers can, however, be easily fooled by the deceptions of a clever patient intent on carrying out a lethal act. The question of how and when to taper precautions can create a dilemma; it is always more desirable to err on the side of caution by sustaining the precautions one month longer than necessary rather than tapering one month too early. To manage this uncertainty, the treating psychiatrist can conduct a review and revise the collaborative care plan during the maintenance phase, based on input from the patient and others in the support system. This input regarding what did or didn't work and how to manage anticipated risks provides the plan for the next episode requiring management of heightened suicidality. During the euthymic state the general maintenance plan can be reviewed with emphasis on the role of continued prophylactic treatment as part of the suicide prevention strategy.

The objectives of the maintenance phase are to sustain wellness and maximize the patient's quality of life. Success of the prophylactic strategy rests heavily on good mood hygiene, a competent support system, and concordance/adherence with the pharmacological regime. Routine follow-up visits include monitoring for treatment adherence, monitoring for impending new episodes, and active management of adverse effects. The risk of self-harm may be reduced by incorporating strategies for recognition and management into a treatment plan, formulated during periods of remission when the patient is less burdened by acute symptoms. In this context, suicidality is discussed as a symptom of the disease rather than a trait of the individual patient and the collaborative care plan is discussed as a means of maintaining the patient's executive control in the face of a disabling episode. A proactive approach taken from the beginning can maximize involvement of family and other significant supports who may provide surrogate executive function for the patient during times of impairment.

Assessment

Integration of suicide prevention into the outpatient management plan starts at the initiation of the treatment relationship and continues at follow-up visits. For patients with mood disorder, every visit can include at least minimal assessment of suicidality. This task can be accomplished in a consistent time-efficient manner by using the "Clinical Self-Report Form" in the waiting room and the "Clinical Monitoring Form" provided in Appendices 1 and 4.

Management Cannot Rely on Scales or Predictors

An appropriate management plan must be formulated in the face of considerable uncertainty. While the research literature has increased our general understanding of risk factors, screening instruments cannot provide sufficient predictive value for clinical use. The problem of prediction becomes truly daunting when the issue is viewed from the perspective of a hypothetical screening instrument. Imagine that a serum suicidality test became available that far exceeds any currently available screening test. If such a test, with 99% sensitivity and 99% specificity, was used to screen one million people in the general population (with a suicide rate of 20/100,000/year), it would detect 198 of the 200 true positive cases. Of the 199,800 true negatives, our serum suicidality test with 99% specificity would yield 1,998 false positives. This means that the accuracy of the positive screening test (predictive power = true positives/total positives) obtained in the 2196 cases with positive screening test results would only be 9% (198/2196). What if our imaginary serum screening test were used only in a very high-risk population? A hypothetical sample of 10,000 with several risk factors, including current hospitalization for a suicide attempt, might have a risk for suicide approaching 1000/100,000 per year. In this instance, predictive value for a positive test would rise to 50% (99 true positives/99 true positives + 99 false positives) for the year (*see* Figure 7.1). The ability to identify patients with these risk factors raises the issue of how to intervene for patients identified as being at high risk. Since our hypothetical screening test results are associated with risk over a one-year period, immediate management presents another dilemma. Hospitalization offers a safer environment, but currently available predictors do not really inform clinical decision making as to when a high-risk patient should be hospitalized nor when discharge is appropriate. Furthermore, sole reliance on hospitalization as the clinical intervention for suicidality may place the patient in a position that discourages open communication.

In the absence of reliable predictors of immediate risk, what can be done for an individual bipolar patient? The STEP-BD Clinical Monitoring Form supports the assessment of suicidality and assignment of standardized quantitative rating (*see* Table 7.6) at every visit. Record keeping conventions for patients at risk recommend a simple routine inquiry to gauge the patient's inclination and opportunity for suicide and documentation of any intervention. For this purpose, inclination describes the degree to which a patient desires to end their life and opportunity refers to the ease to which the patient has access to lethal means. Considering inclination and opportunity separately as dimensions of risk helps to direct the clinician's evaluation of a patient's suicide risk and offers targets for intervention. The outcome of this evaluation structures the first steps

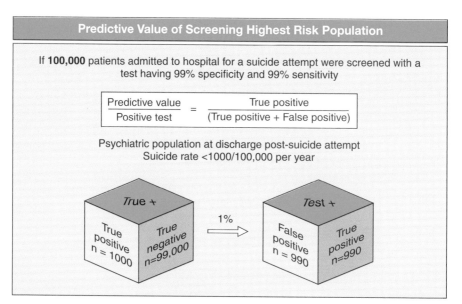

Figure 7.1

Probe Questions and Conventions for Rating Suicidal Ideation on the STEP-BD Clinical Monitoring Form		
Suicidal Ideation: Were there times when you were feeling so bad that you felt life was not worth living? What about actually thinking about suicide or harming yourself? Narrative note required if code >1/4. If passive or active suicidal ideation, document details and plan for safety.		
Suicidal Ideation: Weary of life, would be better off dead, morbid preoccupation, thoughts of harming self, plans for self-destruction, urge to end life. Use narrative note if code >1/4. If passive or active suicidal ideation, document details and plan for safety.		
0	No SI / no morbid preoccupation	
	Frequency	**Intensity**
¼	Rare fleeting	**LNWL** **Passive SI** (Thoughts of death without plan for self destruction, no action or urge to act)
½	Several days, fleeting	**LNWL** **Passive SI** (Thoughts of death without plan for self destruction, no action or urge to act) **Active SI** (Suicidal thoughts with plan for self destruction but no action or urge to act)
	Several days, persistent periods	**Passive SI** (Thoughts of death without plan for self destruction, no action or urge to act)
1 Moderate	Nearly every day, persistent most of the day	**LNWL**
	Nearly every day, persistent periods	**Passive SI** (Thoughts of death without plan for self destruction, no action or urge to act)
	Several days, brief	**Active SI** (Suicidal thoughts with plan for self destruction but no action or urge to act
1.5	>1 Persistent period	**Active SI** (Thoughts of death with plan for self destruction but no action or urge to act)
2 Much more	Nearly every day, persistent	**Active SI** (Thoughts of death with plan for self destruction but no action or urge to act)
	Any	Active SI with urges to harm self or has been self destructive (not superficial gesture)

Table 7.6. SI, suicidal ideation; LNWL, life not worth living.

in the process of formulating clinical interventions matched to the permutations of inclination and opportunity for self-destructive behavior such as indicated in Table 7.7.

Inclination Opportunity Matrix and Some Possible Interventions			
	Opportunity		
	Low No readily available lethal means and frequent close scrutiny	**Moderate** Some lethal means available or frequently alone	**High** Lethal means readily available and frequently alone
High Moderate-severe depression/active suicidal ideation	Treat acute episode consider ECT or medication to reduce SI. Use supports to manage nihilism		Eliminate access to lethal means: hospitalize unless supports are adequate to assure safety
Moderate Mild–moderate depression/ passive suicidal ideation		Reduce access to lethal means: treat current episode	
Low Not acutely depressed, manic, or mixed episode	Avoid unnecessary exposure to lethal means: prophylactic treatment	Avoid unnecessary exposure to lethal means: prophylactic treatment (lithium)	Reduce unnecessary exposure to lethal means: prophylactic treatment (lithium)

(INCLINATION)

Table 7.7. ECT, electroconvulsive therapy; SI, suicidal ideation.

Primary Considerations for Assessment of Inclination and Opportunity

While many factors may contribute to risk of suicide, in the interest of practicality we have narrowed the list to twelve salient items, summarized in Table 7.7. Note that, while half of suicides in bipolar illness occur within six years of onset, the other half can occur at any time and there is no completely safe period. Changes in support systems, health, or substance abuse are only a few of the factors that can increase suicide risk even after many years of illness without suicide attempts.

Interventions

Encourage Incorporation of Specific Harm Reduction Strategies into the Treatment Plan

Since suicide risk reflects both opportunity and inclination, harm reduction strategies can be focused on reducing a patient's access to lethal means (particularly firearms) and ensuring that patients are not isolated. It should be clear to patients that the presence of a lethal means and isolation are associated with an increased risk of self harm. Patients are encouraged to include provisions in their Collaborative Care Plan to automatically increase the frequency of contacts with supports in response to predefined mood states and suicidality.

Determine Follow-Up Interval and Treatment Venue

Local standards and clinician judgment determine acceptable intervals for follow-up. In most circumstances when new medical treatment is initiated, a follow-up interval of one to two weeks is appropriate for managing most outpatients. Patients should know how to reach the clinician in case of emergency. Patients with mild–moderate depression and good support systems may be more safely managed at longer intervals than severely-ill patients who lack reliable supports, but all depressed patients are at risk for self-destructive behavior. Patients with active suicidal ideation or other signs of high inclination warrant aggressive treatment aimed at reducing the depression, and may require hospitalization since none of the currently available antidepressant treatments for outpatients delivers reliable results in less than three weeks, and risk of suicide may increase in early improvement of depression. If measures are taken to adequately monitor the patient and reduce opportunities for self-harm (eg, eliminate access to firearms and other lethal agents), many acutely-depressed patients can be managed without hospitalization. Hospitalization should be offered as a reasonable means of reducing opportunity if:

- suicide is contemplated as a solution to problems;
- the patient is actively planning for death;
- the patient recently made an attempt to end their life;
- no less restrictive option is available offering reasonable safety.

Patients refusing hospitalization can be offered less restrictive treatment under circumstances where supports are able and willing to provide adequate assurance of safety. Involuntary hospitalization can be life-saving when no other reliable means are available to reduce opportunity, but is not in itself treatment, nor does hospitalization assure complete safety. It is, therefore, best to initiate treatment with a follow-up interval which avoids dispensing large amounts of potentially lethal medications (especially lithium and tricyclic antidepressants).

Interventions for Reducing Inclination

Depression is a risk factor for suicide even in patients evidencing no current self-destructive urges. Limiting the quantity of medication prescribed at any one time to amounts that would not be lethal if the entire amount dispensed were ingested does not by itself assure safety, but can lessen one potential source of lethality. Dispensing amounts of medication sufficient to ensure supply to the next appointment may require extra safety measures. Pharmacological interventions have proven efficacious for treatment of depression and mania, and for prophylaxis.

Prophylactic Treatments

Experts generally recommend ongoing prophylactic treatment for bipolar patients in every phase of their illness [26]. Effective prophylactic treatment may reduce the risk of suicide by reducing the recurrence of new episodes, particularly depressive and mixed episodes. Some medication may have specific antisuicide effects independent of their thymoleptic properties. Lithium, for example, reduces the risk of suicide in selected patients from about 30 times to about 6.5 times the risk in the general population [11,12]. This robust reduction (approximately 80%) in risk of suicide, suggests use of lithium as part of the maintenance treatment for bipolar patients in high-risk subgroups. Lithium does not, however, completely eliminate the risk of suicide, and risk of suicide increases in the year after discontinuation of lithium [12]. The benefit of other bimodal maintenance treatments (*see* Chapter 5) is not well established [27], but valproate and lithium appear to reduce suicidal ideation. The sample size requirements virtually preclude a fully-powered randomized investigation of the antisuicide effects of medications. Thies-Flechtner *et al.* randomized 378 bipolar subjects to lithium or carbamazepine. Over a 2.5 year follow-up, significantly more suicidal behavior (nine suicides or suicide attempts) was observed in the group receiving carbamazepine compared with that receiving lithium (zero suicides or suicide attempts) [28], suggesting that lithium may possess antisuicide activity independent of its antidepressant and antimanic effects.

Antidepressants and Electroconvulsive Therapy

There are as yet no data suggesting specific antisuicide benefit for any antidepressant medication in patients with BD [29]. Standard antidepressant agents are, however, effective for treatment of acute depressive episodes, and for this reason may be useful in reducing the heightened inclination associated with depressive episodes. Overall, the efficacy of approved standard antidepressant medications is equivalent [30]. Therefore, the choice of medication for a specific individual is often based on considerations such as adverse-effect profile, allergy, cardiac status, insurance restrictions, cost, and safety in overdose. Tricyclic antidepressants, particularly desipramine, are recognized for their lethality in overdose, and their use requires caution [31–35].

The early phase of recovery is a period of potentially increased risk. Theoretically, suicidal behavior might occur during the resolution of the depressive syndrome, if improvement in psychomotor retardation precedes the lifting of depressive mood, negative cognitions, and perceptual distortion. Rare reports of worsening suicidal ideation during treatment, and meta-analysis of trials presented to the Food and Drug Administration (FDA) – revealing a small but worrisome trend of more suicides among subjects randomized to standard antidepressants as a class and reaching statistical significance for paroxetine-treated subjects – have deepened concerns about antidepressants as an iatrogenic factor in suicide. Currently available data do not support a conclusion that any one drug or subgroup of antidepressant drugs is substantially more likely to worsen suicidal ideation, or induce suicidality, than any other class of antidepressant medication. Therefore, concern about the possibility of treatment-emergent worsening can be included along with other cautions when prescribing antidepressant medications. Patients should be made aware of this small risk in much the same way as information regarding the real but small risk associated with vaccines is routinely communicated in the context of risk:benefit ratios. For patients at high risk, electroconvulsive therapy (ECT) represents the safest, fastest, and most effective treatment option.

Antipsychotic Medication

Even in the absence of frank psychotic symptoms, antipsychotic medications may be useful in reducing acute suicidal ideation. This may reflect their effectiveness in reducing overstimulation. Data from meta-analysis of other trials involving schizophrenic patients indicate that olanzapine, risperidone, and quetiapine may be more beneficial than haloperidol for this purpose [36]. Neuroleptic medications, particularly at high dosage, can increase dysphoria in some patients. Akathisia may contribute dramatic dysphoria which can heighten the motivation for suicide as a mean of eliminating intolerable suffering [37]. Atypical antipsychotic agents are not free of akathisia, but may have less burden in this regard than conventional antipsychotic agents.

In the largest parallel group study ever undertaken to examine specific effects on suicidality, Meltzer *et al.* randomized 985 schizophrenic patients at high risk for suicide to treatment with clozapine or olanzapine. This study found no difference in actual death rates, but overall clozapine treatment was associated with significantly less suicidal behavior [38].

Anxiolytic Agents

Reduction of anxiety may be of benefit in the management of patients with suicidal ideation. Despite their potential for abuse and the possibility of releasing the patient from protective inhibitions, benzodiazepines are often employed as short-term treatment. This class of medication has the advantage of rapid onset, and appears to be reasonably safe when used judiciously. In the absence of a history of drug-induced disinhibition, the risk of harm from acute treatment with benzodiazepines is usually overshadowed by the benefit derived from the remission of overwhelming anxiety.

Verbal Intervention

In addition to pharmacological treatments, psychosocial interventions may also play an important role in the treatment plan; medication effects are not immediate. Adjunctive psychosocial intervention can both augment the medication regimen and provide immediate management of suicidal urges. This intervention plays a key role in the plan to assure safety, particularly during the lag phase before antidepressants become effective. However, psychotherapy should not be expected to cure suicidal ideation. Realistically, psychotherapy aims to achieve the more modest specific objectives of decreasing inclination, reducing isolation, and helping the patient and support members activate protective factors of the treatment contract.

While psychotherapy during acute periods of suicidal ideation can help both patient and family to minimize inclination and opportunity, it might be most helpful during periods of wellness. During this time, a treatment contract can be developed to help protect the patient. Specific forms of psychotherapy that have been used in BD are cognitive-behavioral therapy (CBT) [18,1939–42], family focused therapy (FFT) [20,21], and interpersonal and social rhythm therapy (IPSRT) [15,22,23].

Acknowledgement of suicidal ideation is an important element of any mode of therapy utilized to reduce suicidality. Elements of these formal therapies can be incorporated in the routine psychotherapeutic approach used by treating psychiatrists who carry out clinical management without traditional psychotherapy. Yet it can be difficult for clinicians and family members to sustain participation when patients talk persistently about their suicidal thoughts. Even the most caring supports may respond to the chronic expression of nihilism in an unconstructive manner, especially when several treatment options have been tried without success; care providers demoralized by the patient's lack of progress may find themselves agreeing with the patient's hopelessness. Others may cope by attempting to ignore or avoid the individual. The shortcomings of these strategies are obvious. Constructing a long contingency list of potential treatments and scheduling time (eg, 15–60 minutes per day) for the patient to express nihilism and discuss suicidal ideation, may offer a more sustainable and safer alternative plan for maintaining therapeutic optimism. Supports can learn to acknowledge the patient's hopelessness as a feeling state, while gently questioning its standing as an unchangeable reality. This plan provides the patient with the assurance of being heard and reduces the widespread fear among supports that once started, conversation will lead to an endless downward spiral. Clinical experience suggests that setting time boundaries is effective in managing inclination and progressing to activities that will further decrease suicidal behaviors. In practice, this strategy also restores the opportunity for supports to structure the patient's time with distractions more pleasurable than spending time ruminating on aspects of a life that appears not to be worth living.

Reduce Access to Lethal Means and Avoid Social Isolation

A patient's opportunity to act on suicidal ideation can be reduced by removing access to lethal means and minimizing the time spent in isolation. Any guns and other weapons easily available to the patient should be put under the control of reliable others. A reduction in a patient's inclination for suicide can be a more daunting task for clinicians and support members. Following acknowledgement of suicidal thought, reminding the patient that suicide is not the final answer may be effective in lessening suicidal ideation, and discourse should be redirected towards alternative ways of resolving threatening situations. Remaining mindful of positive aspects in a patient's life can be a key to sustaining hope during times of heightened suicidality.

Summary

The risk of suicide in bipolar patients is high and can be reduced by treatment. Despite the identification of numerous risk factors there is no clinically useful screening tool to determine immediate individual risk and no means of guaranteeing absolute long-term safety. Although much of what is suggested above is offered in the absence of evidence, there are many opportunities to integrate practical, low-cost suicide prevention strategies into the outpatient treatment plan for bipolar patients. The three basic elements are:

1) routine assessment of inclination and opportunity for suicide;

2) education of patient and family regarding risk factors; and

3) integration of suicide prevention strategies into a written treatment plan.

Well-intentioned recommendations for education of patients and supports can have greater impact when translated into practical, written, time-efficient procedures. Use of written materials like the STEP-BD Collaborative Care Workbook can aid the patient and treatment team by providing enduring reference materials and fostering the development of a personalized written treatment plan. Knowledge of risk and protective factors, and identification and empowerment of supports who can act as surrogates performing executive functions at times when illness diminishes the patient's capacity, are central to a successful treatment plan.

References

1. Akiskal HS, Maser JD, Zeller PJ *et al.* **Switching from 'unipolar' to bipolar II. An 11-year prospective study of clinical and temperamental predictors in 559 patients.** *Arch Gen Psychiatry* 1995; **52**:114–123.

2. National Institute of Mental Health. *NIMH - Suicide Facts.* Bethesda: National Institute of Mental Health, 2002.

3. Shaffer D, Craft L. **Methods of adolescent suicide prevention.** *J Clin Psychiatry* 1999; **60**(Suppl 2):70–74; discussion 75–6, 113–116.

4. Goodwin FK, Jamison K. *Manic Depressive Illness.* New York: Oxford University Press, 1990.

5. Isometsa ET. **Psychological autopsy studies – a review.** *Eur Psychiatry* 2001; **16**:379–385.

6. Isometsa ET, Lonnqvist JK. **Suicide attempts preceding completed suicide.** *Br J Psychiatry* 1998; **173**:531–535.

7. Tsuang MT. **Suicide in schizophrenics, manics, depressives, and surgical controls. A comparison with general population suicide mortality.** *Arch Gen Psychiatry* 1978; **35**:153–155.

8. Weeke A, Kastrup M, Dupont A. **Long-stay patients in Danish psychiatric hospitals.** *Psychol Med* 1979; **9**:551–566.

9. Hunt IM, Robinson M, Bickley H *et al.* **Suicides in ethnic minorities within 12 months of contact with mental health services. National clinical survey.** *Br J Psychiatry* 2003; **183**:155–160.

10. Angst J, Angst F, Stassen HH. **Suicide risk in patients with major depressive disorder.** *J Clin Psychiatry* 1999; **60**(Suppl 2):57–62; discussion 75–6, 113–116.

11. Angst F, Stassen HH, Clayton PJ *et al.* **Mortality of patients with mood disorders: follow-up over 34–38 years.** *J Affect Disord* 2002; **68**:167–181.

12. Tondo L, Baldessarini RJ, Hennen J *et al.* **Lithium treatment and risk of suicidal behavior in bipolar disorder patients.** *J Clin Psychiatry* 1998; **59**:405–414.

13. Tondo L, Baldessarini RJ, Floris G. **Long-term clinical effectiveness of lithium maintenance treatment in types I and II bipolar disorders.** *Br J Psychiatry Suppl* 2001; **41**:s184–190.

14. Sachs GS, Yan LJ, Swann AC *et al.* **Integration of suicide prevention into outpatient management of bipolar disorder.** *J Clin Psychiatry* 2001; **62**(Suppl 25):3–11.

15. Frank E, Novick D. **Progress in the psychotherapy of mood disorders: studies from the Western Psychiatric Institute and Clinic.** *Epidemiol Psichiatr Soc* 2001; **10**:245–252.

16. Post RM, Rubinow PR, Uhde TW *et al.* **Dysphoric mania. Clinical and biological correlates.** *Arch Gen Psychiatry* 1989; **46**:353–358.

17. Runeson B, Asberg M. **Family history of suicide among suicide victims.** *Am J Psychiatry* 2003; **160**:1525–1526.

18. Craighead WE, Miklowitz DJ. **Psychosocial interventions for bipolar disorder.** *J Clin Psychiatry* 2000; **61**(Suppl 13):58–64.

19. Scott J. **Psychotherapy for bipolar disorder.** *Br J Psychiatry* 1995; **167**:581–588.

20. Miklowitz DJ, Richards JA, George EL *et al.* **Integrated family and individual therapy for bipolar disorder: results of a treatment development study.** *J Clin Psychiatry* 2003; **64**:182–191.

21. Miklowitz DJ, George EL, Richard JA *et al.* **A randomized study of family-focused psychoeducation and pharmacotherapy in the outpatient management of bipolar disorder.** *Arch Gen Psychiatry* 2003; **60**:904–912.

22. Frank E, Swartz HA, Kupfer DJ. **Interpersonal and social rhythm therapy: managing the chaos of bipolar disorder.** *Biol Psychiatry* 2000; **48**:593–604.

23. Frank E, Grochocinski VJ, Spanier CA *et al.* **Interpersonal psychotherapy and antidepressant medication: evaluation of a sequential treatment strategy in women with recurrent major depression.** *J Clin Psychiatry* 2000; **61**:51–57.

24. Otto MW, Reilly-Harrington N, Sachs G. *Collaborative Care Handbook: A Workbook for Individuals and Families.* Boston: Massachusetts General Hospital, 1999.

25. Suicide Prevention and Depressive Disorders, 1993 report from National Depressive and Manic Depressive Association, Chicago.

26. Bowden CL, Lecrubier Y, Bauer M *et al.* **Maintenance therapies for classic and other forms of bipolar disorder.** *J Affect Disord* 2000; **59**(Suppl 1):S57–S67.

27. Bowden CL. **The ability of lithium and other mood stabilizers to decrease suicide risk and prevent relapse.** *Curr Psychiatry Rep* 2000; **2**:490–494.

28. Thies-Flechtner K, Muller-Oerlinghausen B, Seibert W *et al.* **Effect of prophylactic treatment on suicide risk in patients with major affective disorders. Data from a randomized prospective trial.** *Pharmacopsychiatry* 1996; **29**:103–107.

29. Khan A, Khan S, Kolts R *et al.* **Suicide rates in clinical trials of SSRIs, other antidepressants, and placebo: analysis of FDA reports.** *Am J Psychiatry* 2003; **160**:790–792.

30. Frank E, Karp JF, Rush AJ. **Efficacy of treatments for major depression.** *Psychopharmacol Bull* 1993; **29**:457–475.

31. Kapur N, House A, May C *et al.* **Service provision and outcome for deliberate self-poisoning in adults – results from a six centre descriptive study.** *Soc Psychiatry Psychiatr Epidemiol* 2003; **38**:390–395.

32. Crome P, Ali C. **Clinical features and management of self-poisoning with newer antidepressants.** *Med Toxicol* 1986; **1**:411–420.

33. Crome P. **The toxicity of drugs used for suicide.** *Acta Psychiatr Scand Suppl* 1993; **371**:33–37.

34. Crome P. **Antidepressant poisoning.** *Acta Psychiatr Scand Suppl* 1983; **302**:95–101.

35. Freemantle N, House A, Song F *et al.* **Prescribing selective serotonin reuptake inhibitors as strategy for prevention of suicide.** *Br Med J* 1994; **309**:249–253.

36. Meltzer HY. **Treatment of suicidality in schizophrenia.** *Ann NY Acad Sci* 2001; **932**:44–58; discussion 58–60.

37. Drake RE, Ehrlich J. **Suicide attempts associated with akathisia.** *Am J Psychiatry* 1985; **142**:499–501.

38. Meltzer HY, Alphs L, Green AI *et al.* **Clozapine treatment for suicidality in schizophrenia: International Suicide Prevention Trial (InterSePT).** *Arch Gen Psychiatry* 2003; **60**:82–91.

39. Otto MW, Reilly-Harrington N, Sachs GS. **Psychoeducational and cognitive-behavioral strategies in the management of bipolar disorder.** *J Affect Disord* 2003; **73**:171–181.

40. Scott J. **Cognitive therapy of affective disorders: a review.** *J Affect Disord* 1996; **37**:1–11.

41. Scott J. **Group psychoeducation reduces recurrence and hospital admission in people with bipolar disorder.** *Evid Based Ment Health* 2003; **6**:115.

42. Lam DH, Watkins ER, Hayward P *et al.* **A randomized controlled study of cognitive therapy for relapse prevention for bipolar affective disorder: outcome of the first year.** *Arch Gen Psychiatry* 2003; **60**:145–152.

Chapter 8

Practical Therapeutics

In addition to an understanding of the evidence supporting the use of specific agents at key decision points, medication management requires a grasp of the practical details related to prescribing and pharmacology. This chapter outlines practical information related to the use of 11 agents defined as first-line treatment in the clinical pathways. Additional information is offered to guide the use of other commonly prescribed medications.

The collaborative process of selecting treatment for an individual patient proceeds in three basic steps. First, a review of the overall menu of reasonable choices – the first-line evidence-based treatments described in the preceding chapters – for each decision point. Next, the treating clinician considers the appropriateness of each item on the overall menu (based on individual factors), and by culling out those agents judged ineffective, intolerable, or inappropriate creates an individualized menu of reasonable choices. Finally, this menu, along with the profiles of each agent, is presented to the patient, who makes a choice based on their perception of the relative desirability of the alternatives offered.

Classify Treatments Based on Efficacy, Tolerability, and Mechanism

The term "mood stabilizer" has been widely accepted and appears frequently in psychiatric literature, despite the absence of a consensus definition. Though conceptually appealing, the "mood stabilizer" classification is difficult to define in scientific terms and often contributes to misunderstanding between patient and doctor.

If the designation "mood stabilizer" were reserved for therapies demonstrating efficacy in double-blind trials for all four of the primary therapeutic objectives, even lithium might not meet the full criteria to be included in this category. Even if such a definition were not overly restrictive, the term "mood stabilizer" is impractical because it obscures the relevant psychotropic properties of the treatment.

For purposes of clarity, it is practical to refer to treatments based on their proven efficacy and designate as first-line those with category A evidence and a desirable tolerability profile. Second-line agents would be category A therapies limited by tolerability issues, as well as treatments with positive findings at levels of evidence category B and category C. All treatment with lesser evidence should be considered unproven exploratory options. Even when category A evidence suggests a clear class effect, other agents in the class should be held in reserve for use only when proven alternative agents are rejected, unavailable, or poorly tolerated.

Antimanic

The first-line antimanic category would include nine agents: six dopamine blocking agents (aripiprazole, haloperidol, olanzapine, quetiapine, risperidone, ziprasidone), and three nondopamine-blocking antimanic agents (lithium, valproate, carbamazepine).

Beyond this, treatments such as topiramate, oxcarbazepine, and other dopamine-blocking agents could be considered as second-line members of the antimanic treatment category based on inconsistent results, unconvincing evidence, or class effects.

Bipolar Antidepressant

First-line treatment for bipolar depression would include three options: lamotrigine, fluoxetine combined with olanzapine, and olanzapine alone – all agents with proven efficacy for bipolar depression. Within the bipolar antidepressant category, agents (as a class) with proven efficacy in unipolar depression, grouped as standard antidepressants, meet criteria for second-line use.

Prophylactic Agents

First-line agents for prevention of relapse would include lamotrigine, lithium, olanzapine, and valproate. Ideally, treatment for bipolar disorder (BD) would have prophylactic as well as acute efficacy. Treatments with proven efficacy for mania, depression, or prophylaxis are considered to have bimodal activity. Therapies shown to be effective for one or more of the primary therapeutic objectives may offer valuable mood stabilization to bipolar patients, as long as they can be administered without the risk of exacerbating the illness.

For any patient, a first-line mood stabilizer would be one that had a desirable safety profile and reasonable efficacy. In practice, this means there is no individual contraindication (eg, known hypersensitivity), the potential for intolerable effects (eg, seizure, coma, death) is very low, and the tolerability of the expectable adverse effects is very high. In the United States, the Food and Drug Administration (FDA) has granted approval to lithium, divalproex, and olanzapine for the treatment of mania. In Europe, lithium and carbamazepine have regulatory approval.

Abbreviations for drug tables

ACE-I	angiotensin-converting enzyme inhibitor
AIMS	abnormal involuntary movement scale
AV	atrioventricular
BUN	blood urea nitrogen
Ca^{2+} blockers	calcium-channel blockers
CBZ	carbamazepine
CNS	central nervous system
Chol	cholesterol
CBC	complete blood count
diff	differential
EKG	electrocardiogram
EPS	extrapyramidal side effects
GI	gastrointestinal
H2 blockers	histamine 2 blockers
LFT	liver function tests
MAO-I	monoamine oxidase inhibitor
MHD	monohydroxy derivative
MI	myocardial infarction
NA	narrow angle
NMS	neuroleptic malignant syndrome
NSAIDS	non-steroidal anti-inflammatory drugs
Se	selenium
SSRIs	selective serotonin reuptake inhibitors
TFT	thyroid function tests
TG	triglycerides
Zn	zinc

Nondopamine-Blocking Drugs Commonly Used for Bipolar Disorder

Carbamazepine

Approved indications	Epilepsy, trigeminal neuralgia (mania, expected 2004)
Warnings	Impairment of cardiac, renal, or liver function. Prior hematological dyscrasia. History of bone marrow depression. Sensitivity to tricyclic compounds or MAO-I
Drug interactions	**Induces:** P450, CYP 3A4. **Reduces:** neuroleptic levels, oral contraceptive, CBZ, many others. **Increased by:** H2 blockers, nefazodone, erythromycin, isoniazid, propoxyphene, valproate, Ca^{2+} blockers, lithium. CYP 3A4 inhibitors (eg, nefazodone) inhibit CBZ metabolism, CYP 3A4 inducers increase CBZ metabolism.
Most common adverse effects	CNS: dizziness, sedation, unsteady gait, cognitive impairment, blurred vision/diplopia, elevated liver function tests. GI: nausea, anorexia, pain, vomiting.
Most worrisome adverse effects	Aplastic anemia, agranulocytosis, thrombocytopenia, hepatitis. Skin: rash (pruritic, erythematous), erythema multiforme or nodosum, toxic epidermal necrolysis, Stevens-Johnson. Other: hyponatremia, altered thyroid function, edema, arrhythmia, AV block, alopecia, systemic lupus erythematosis, potential teratogen.
Initiation/maintenance treatment	**Initial dosage:** 200 mg bid/tid. **More gradual titration can minimize side effects:** 200 mg qhs x 2 days; 400 mg qhs x 2 days; 200 mg qam/400 mg qhs x 2 days then 400 mg bid; titrate to clinical response, not level.
Laboratories	**Pretreatment:** CBC diff, platelets, LFT, urinalysis. Useful: EKG, electrolytes, reticulocyte count. **Follow-up:** every 7–14 days: CBC, drug level, LFT for 2–3 months and stable dose. **Routine** (monthly x 4 months): drug level, CBC, LFT, electrolytes. Thereafter, every 6–12 months: CBC, drug level, LFT, electrolytes, TFT.

Patient education

Expect: sedation, GI symptoms, lightheadedness.
Report: rash, jaundice, incoordination, irregular heartbeat, facial edema.
Be aware of: importance of weight control program, common drug interactions, potential teratogenicity, use of vitamins/minerals (folate, Se, Zn).

Gabapentin

Approved indications	Adjunctive treatment for partial seizures in adults, no bipolar indication
Warnings	Impairment of liver or kidney function.
Drug interactions	Antacids.
Most common adverse effects	Somnolence, ataxia, fatigue, nystagmus. CNS: dizziness, sedation, unsteady gait, incoordination, cognitive impairment, blurred vision/diplopia, elevated LFT. GI: nausea, anorexia, pain.
Most worrisome adverse effects	Worsening mania. Other: hair loss, weight gain, teratogenicity (category C).
Initiation/maintenance treatment	**Initial dosage:** 300–600 mg aq x 3–5 days then increase daily dose by 300–600 mg each week. **Usual maintenance:** 900–3600 mg. More gradual titration may be necessary for some patients.
Laboratories	None required. **Required pretreatment:** CBC + diff, platelets, LFT, urinalysis. **Useful:** EKG, electrolytes.
Patient education	**Expect:** sedation, GI symptoms, lightheadedness. **Report:** rash, incoordination. **Be aware of:** importance of weight control program, common drug interactions, potential teratogenicity, use of vitamins/minerals (folate, Se, Zn).

Lamotrigine

Approved indications	Epilepsy, bipolar maintenance.
Warnings	Impairment of liver or kidney function.
Drug interactions	**Increase lamotrigine levels:** valproic acid. **Decrease lamictal levels:** phenytoin, phenobarbital, primidone, CBZ, phenytoin, folate inhibitors.
Most common adverse effects	Ataxia, dizziness, sedation, insomnia, nausea/vomiting.
Most worrisome adverse effects	Stevens-Johnson. Other important: rash, blurred vision, diplopia, esophagitis, teratogenicity (category C).
Initiation/maintenance treatment	**Initial dosage:** 25 mg qd x 1–2 weeks; 50 mg qd x 1 week; 75 mg qd x 1 week; 100 mg qd x 1 week; then increase daily dose 50 mg each week to usual maintenance dose 100–200 mg. **If concurrent valproate:** 25 mg qod x 2 weeks; 25 mg qd x 2 weeks; do not exceed 150 mg/day
Laboratories	None required. Potentially useful if concurrent with drugs that alter metabolism: serum levels, LFT, CBC.
Patient education	**Expect** (transiently): insomnia, sedation, nausea, dizziness. **Report:** rash. **Be aware of:** common drug interactions, potential teratogenicity.

Lithium

Approved indications	Bipolar mania. Maintenance therapy for bipolar disorder.
Warnings	Renal impairment, cardiovascular disease, complicated fluid or salt balance, acute MI, myasthenia gravis, pregnancy.
Drug interactions	Diuretics, NSAIDS, CBZ, Ca^{2+} blockers, ACE-I, metronidazole, neuroleptics.
Most common adverse effects	GI irritation, sedation, tremor. Other: weight gain, edema, acne, psoriasis, polyuria, polydipsia.
Most worrisome adverse effects	Acute intoxication: seizure, coma, death. Intoxication sequelae: renal, cardiac, CNS. Other: thyroid inhibition, arrhythmias, renal dysfunction, teratogenicity.
Initiation/maintenance treatment	**Initial dosage:** 300–450 mg bid, then titrate to therapeutic range or highest dose tolerated. **More gradual titration can minimize side effects:** 300 mg qhs x 2 days; 600 mg qhs x 2 days; 300 mg qam and 600 mg qhs x 2 days, then 600 mg bid.
Laboratories	**Pretreatment:** CBC, electrolytes, thyroid, creatinine, BUN, urinalysis, EKG if >35 or clinically indicated. **When stable:** lithium level 1–4 months for 1 year Every 6–12 months or when clinically indicated: lithium level, TFT, creatinine, BUN, urinalysis, CBC.
Patient education	**Expect** (one or more): GI irritation, sedation, mild tremor, thirst, increased white blood count. **Report:** moderate tremor, slurred speech, muscle twitching, change in fluid balance, impaired memory, rash, edema. **Be aware of:** lab rationale, weight control, importance of sodium, potential teratogenicity.

Oxcarbazepine

Approved indications	Epilepsy (Adjunctive treatment for partial seizures). No bipolar indication.
Warnings	Impairment of liver or kidney function.
Drug interactions	T½ oxcarbazepine = 1–2.5 hours, T½ MHD (an active metabolite) ~ 9 hours, induces P450 CYP 3A4. **Reduces:** antipsychotic levels, oral contraceptive, CBZ, many others. **Increased by:** H2 blockers, nefazodone, erythromycin, isoniazid, propoxyphene, valproate, Ca^{2+} blockers, lithium.
Most common adverse effects	Sedation, headache, dizziness, asthenia, tremor, ataxia, nausea, difficulty concentrating.
Most worrisome adverse effects	Other: abdominal pain, confusion – teratogenicity (category C).
Initiation/maintenance treatment	**Initial dosage:** 4 mg qd x 5–7 days then titrate daily treatment dose 150 mg each week to clinical effect or highest dose tolerated. **Sequential care:** 150 mg qhs x 2 days; 300 mg qhs x 2 days; 150 mg qam/300 mg qhs x 2 days then 300 bid. Titrate to clinical response, not level. **Urgent care:** not recommended.
Laboratories	**Pretreatment:** CBC + diff, platelets, LFT, urinalysis. Useful: EKG, electrolytes, reticulocyte count. **Follow-up:** every 7–28 days: CBC, drug level, LFT for 2–3 months, and stable dose. Routine (monthly x 4 months): drug level, CBC, LFT, electrolytes. Thereafter, every 6–12 months: CBC, drug level, LFT, electrolytes, TFT.
Patient education	**Expect** (transiently): insomnia/sedation, nausea, dizziness. **Report:** easy bruisability, rash, jaundice, edema (facial). **Be aware of:** common drug interactions, potential teratogenicity, use of vitamins/minerals.

Topiramate

Approved indications	Epilepsy (adjunctive therapy for adults with partial seizures).
Warnings	Impairment of liver or kidney function.
Drug interactions	Decrease topiramate: phenytoin, CBZ, valproate. Cause decrease of: oral contraceptive pill, acetazolamide, dichlorphenamide.
Most common adverse effects	CNS: somnolence, dizziness, anxiety, ataxia, speech disorder, psychomotor slowing, confusion. GI: weight loss, anorexia.
Most worrisome adverse effects	Renal stones, depression.
Initiation/maintenance treatment	**Initial dosage:** inpatient: 50 mg, then increase by 50 mg each day to therapeutic effect or highest tolerated dose. **Outpatient:** 50 mg qd x 7 days, then increase daily dose 50 mg each week. **Usual dose:** acute mania, 200–800 mg; maintenance, 100–600 mg; more gradual titration is necessary for some patients.
Laboratories	**Pretreatment:** none required. Potentially useful: serum levels, LFT, CBC. **Maintenance:** none required. Useful: urinalysis, electrolytes, creatinine.
Patient education	**Expect:** sedation, GI symptoms, lightheadedness. **Report:** rash, jaundice, incoordination, irregular heartbeat, facial edema. **Be aware of:** drug interactions, potential teratogenicity, use of vitamins/minerals (folate, Se, Zn).

Valproate

Approved indications	Bipolar mania, prophylaxis of migraine headaches, reduce incidence of complex partial seizures.
Warnings	Impairment of liver function, blood dyscrasia.
Drug interactions	**Increased GI levels:** aspirin, felbamate, rifampin. **Decreased levels:** CBZ, clonazepam (rare) – absence status. **Inhibits:** diazepam, lamotrigine, phenobarbitol, phenytoin. **Weak inhibition:** P450 isoenzymes.
Most common adverse effects	Tremor, dizziness, sedation, nausea/vomiting, GI pain, headache, elevated LFT, somnolence, asthenia, dyspepsia, rash.
Most worrisome adverse effects	Marrow suppression, thrombocytopenia, prolongation of coagulation time, pancreatitis. Other: hair loss, weight gain, teratogenicity, possible association with polycystic ovarian syndrome.
Initiation/maintenance treatment	**Initial dose:** 250–500 mg bid, more gradual titration can minimize side effects: 250 mg qhs x 2 days; 500 mg qhs x 2 days; 250 mg/500 mg qhs x 2 days then 500 bid. **Alternative rapid titration:** day 1 single dose 20 mg/kg; day 2–4 split bid; day 4 serum level; day 5 adjust as required for valproate = 80 mg/ml; if no improvement in 2 weeks, increase as necessary for valproate = 100 mg/ml.
Laboratories	**Pretreatment:** CBC with diff, platelets, LFT. **Follow-up:** establish level 50–100 mg/l, weekly until stable drug level, CBC and LFT, monthly until 6 months, thereafter every 6–12 months.
Patient education	**Expect** (transiently): sedation, tremor, GI symptoms. **Report:** easy bruisability, abdominal swelling, rash, jaundice, edema (facial). **Be aware of:** weight control program, common drug interactions, potential teratogenicity, use of vitamins/minerals (folate, Se, Zn).

Dopamine-Blocking Drugs Commonly Used for Bipolar Disorder

Comparisons of dopamine-blocking drugs commonly used for BD are shown in Table 8.1.

Dopamine-Blocking Drugs Commonly Used for Bipolar Disorder								
Drug	Sed	WG	AC	HypoT	EPS	Advantages	Disadvantages	USD (mg)
Haloperidol	+	+	-	+	+++	Potency, little hypotension, available IM, IV & elixir	EPS	2–5 qhs
Clozapine	+++	+++	++	++	-	Low incidence EPS, effective in treatment, refractory illness	CBC required (bone marrow suppression), lowers SZ threshold, drug interactions, weight gain, diabetes	50–100 qhs
Risperidone	+	+	-	++	++	Potency, reduced risk EPS, little hypotension, ?antidepressant effect elixir available, long-acting injectable	Prolactin elevation	1–2 qhs
Olanzapine	+++	+++	++	+++	+	Sedating, reduced risk of EPS, modest antidepressant effect	Weight gain, diabetes, lower SZ threshold	5–15 qhs
Quetiapine	++	++	-	+++	-	Sedating, lowest risk of EPS, moderate antidepressant effect	40% reduced clearance in elderly, hypotension, possible development of cataracts (in beagle dogs)	25–300 qhs
Ziprasidone	+/-	-	-	++	++	Nonsedating at low dose, ?antidepressant effect, IM available, weight gain rare	Activation/agitation, less predictable adverse effect pattern	40 bid
Aripiprazole	+/-	-	-	++	+	Usually nonsedating ?antidepressant effect, weight gain rare, long half-life	Activation/agitation, less predictable adverse effect pattern, long half-life	10–15 qam

Table 8.1. AC, anticholinergic; CBC, complete blood count; EPS, extrapyramidal side effects; HypoT, hypotension; IM, intramuscular; IV, intravenous; qam, every morning; qhs, every night at bedtime; Sed, sedation; SZ, seizure; USD, usual starting dose; WG, weight gain; - none/infrequent; +, common; ++, frequent; +++, most frequent; ?, questionable/possible.

Atypical Dopamine-Blocking Agents:

Aripiprazole

Approved indications	Agitation, hallucinations, delusions, paranoia (mania, expected 2004).
Warnings	Seizure disorder, severe akathisia – history of NMS.
Drug interactions	**1° metabolism** – CYP 2D6, CYP 3A4. Serum T½ ~ 75–94 hours (aripiprazole and dehydro-aripiprazole) **Increased by:** inhibition of 2D6, quinidine (+112%), fluoxetine or paroxetine or 3A4 ketoconazole (+70%), nefazodone. **Decreased by:** inducers of 3A4, CBZ (–70%).
Most common adverse effects	Headache, dizziness, postural hypotension, sedation, insomnia, agitation, akathisia, rhinitis, weight gain, EPS, photosensitivity, hyperprolactinemia.
Most worrisome adverse effects	NMS, seizures, acute dystonia, tardive dyskinesia, parkinsonism, priapism. Endocrine: temp dysregulation. GI: dysphagia, teratogenicity (category C).
Initiation/maintenance treatment	**Initial dosage:** 5–15 mg qd. **Maintenance treatment:** 7.5–30 mg qd. **Sequential care:** 5–10 mg x 1–14 days; 10–5 mg x 7–1 days; 15–20 mg x 14–35 days; 20–30 mg x 21–35 days; titrate to clinical response, not dose or level. **Urgent care:** 15– 30 mg x 1–7 days; 20–30 mg x 3– 14 days; usual effective range 15–30 mg/day (mania).
Laboratories	**Pretreatment:** none required. Useful: CBC + diff, electrolytes, LFT, EKG, AIMS, prolactin level. **Follow-up:** none required. Useful: CBC + diff, electrolytes, LFT, EKG, AIMS.
Patient education	**Expect** (at least transiently): one or more of: sedation, headache, dry mouth/constipation, tremor/muscle

stiffness, lightheadedness.

Report: severe tremor/rigidity, rash; persistent sore throat/fever, jaundice, akathisia.

Be aware of: drug interactions, potential for diabetes, potential for tardive dyskinesia.

Olanzapine

Approved indications	Agitation, hallucinations, delusions, paranoia, mania, bipolar maintenance, nausea.
Warnings	Seizure disorder, anticholinergic delirium.
Drug interactions	**1° metabolism** – CYP 1A2, minor 2D6, serum T½ ~ 21–54 hrs, T½ likely reduced by inducers (CBZ, phenobarbital, omeprazole, rifampin) and smoking, T½ increased by inhibitors (fluvoxamine), anticholinergics.
Most common adverse effects	Sedation, headache, weight gain, anticholinergic, alpha blockade, photosensitivity. EPS: parkinsonism, akathisia. Elevation of: Chol, TG.
Most worrisome adverse effects	NMS, seizures, diabetes, tardive dyskinesia, priapism, hematological, teratogenicity (category C). Endocrine: temp dysregulation, NA glaucoma. GI: dysphagia.

Initiation/maintenance treatment

Initial dosage: 5–10 mg qhs.
Maintenance treatment: 2.5–20 mg qhs.
Sequential care: 5–10 mg qd x 1–14 days;
            10–20 mg qd x d 7–21;
            15–30 mg qd x 14–35 days;
            titrate to clinical response, not dose or level.
Urgent care: 10–20 mg x 3–7 days;
            15–30 mg x 3–28 days;
            usual effective range 10–30 mg/day.

Laboratories

Pretreatment: none required.
Useful: weight, glucose, CBC + diff, electrolytes, LFT, Chol, TG, EKG, AIMS.
Follow-up: required: weight.
Useful: glucose, CBC + diff, electrolytes, LFT, Chol, TG.

Patient education

Expect (at least transiently): One or more of: sedation, dry mouth/constipation, headache, tremor/muscle stiffness, lightheadedness, weight gain.
Report: severe tremor/rigidity, rash; persistent sore throat/fever, jaundice, akathisia.
Be aware of: drug interactions, potential for diabetes, potential for tardive dyskinesia.

Quetiapine

Approved indications	Agitation, hallucinations, delusions, paranoia, mania.
Warnings	Seizure disorder, anticholinergic delirium.
Drug interactions	**1° metabolism** – CYP 3A4, serum T½ ~ 6 hours. **T½ increased by:** inhibition of CYP 3A4, ketoconazole, itraconazole, fluconazole, erythromycin. **T½ decreased by:** induction of CYP 3A4, CBZ, phenobarbital. Serum levels increased by: CYP 3A4 inhibition, hepatic impairment, elderly.
Most common adverse effects	Headache, constipation, dizziness, postural hypotension, sedation, weight gain, photosensitivity, sweating. Elevation of: Chol, TG.
Most worrisome adverse effects	NMS, seizures, tardive dyskinesia, priapism, teratogenicity (category C). Endocrine: temp dysregulation, NA glaucoma, cataracts. GI: dysphagia.

Initiation/maintenance treatment

Initial Dosage: 25–100 mg qhs.
Maintenance treatment: 25–600 mg qhs, can split dose bid or tid.
Sequential care: 25–100 mg x 1–14 days;
50–200 mg x 7–21 days;
100–400 mg x 14–35 days;
200–600 mg x 21–35 days;
titrate to clinical response, not dose or level.
Urgent care: 200–300 mg x 3–7 days;
400–600 mg x 3–14 days;
600–800 mg x 9–21 days;
usual effective range 400–800 mg/day.

Laboratories

Pretreatment: required: eye exam.
Useful: weight, glucose, CBC + diff, electrolytes, LFT, thyroid stimulating hormone, Chol, TG, EKG AIMS.
Follow-up: required: q - 6–12 months weight, eye exam.
Useful: glucose, CBC + diff, electrolytes, LFT, thyroid stimulating hormone, Chol, TG.

Patient education

Expect (at least transiently): one or more of: sedation, headache, dry mouth/constipation, tremor/muscle stiffness, lightheadedness.

121

Report: severe tremor/rigidity, rash; persistent sore throat/fever, jaundice, akathisia.

Be aware of: drug interactions, potential for tardive dyskinesia.

Risperidone

Approved indications	Agitation, hallucinations, delusions, paranoia, mania, nausea.
Warnings	Seizure disorder, severe akathisia, history of NMS.
Drug interactions	**1° metabolism** – CYP 2D6, serum T½ ~ 20 hours. T½ **Increased by:** inhibition of 2D6, quinidine, fluoxetine, paroxetine. **T½ reduced by:** CBZ, phenytoin, rifampin, phenobarbital.
Most common adverse effects	Headache, sedation, dizziness, postural hypotension, rhinitis, weight gain, EPS, akathisia, photosensitivity, hyperprolactinemia.
Most worrisome adverse effects	NMS, seizures, acute dystonia, tardive dyskinesia, parkinsonism, priapism, teratogenicity (category C). Endocrine: temp dysregulation. GI: dysphagia.
Initiation/maintenance treatment	**Initial Dosage:** 0.5–1.0 mg qhs. **Maintenance treatment:** 0.5–4 mg qhs. **Sequential care:** 0.5–1 mg x 1–14 days; 1–2 mg x 7–21 days; 2–3 mg x 14–35 days; 3–4 mg x 21–35 days; titrate to clinical response, not dose or level. **Urgent care:** 1–4 mg x 1–7 days; 2–8 mg x 3–14 days; usual effective range 1–4 mg/day.
Laboratories	**Pretreatment:** none required. **Useful:** CBC + diff, electrolytes, LFT, EKG, AIMS, prolactin level. **Follow-up:** none required. Useful: weight, CBC + diff, electrolytes, LFT, EKG, AIMS.
Patient education	**Expect** (at least transiently): one or more of: sedation, headache, dry mouth/constipation, tremor/muscle stiffness, lightheadedness. **Report:** severe tremor/rigidity, rash; persistent sore throat/fever, jaundice, akathisia. **Be aware of:** drug interactions, potential for tardive dyskinesia.

Ziprasidone

Approved indications	Agitation, hallucinations, delusions, paranoia, (mania, expected 2004).
Warnings	Seizure disorder, severe akathisia, history of NMS.
Drug interactions	**1° metabolism (3 routes):** 2/3 – aldehyde oxidase, 1/3 – CYP 3A4, serum T½ ~ 4–7 hours. **Increased by:** inhibition of CYP 3A4 (ketoconazole 35%). **Decreased by:** induction of CYP 3A4 (CBZ 35%).
Most common adverse effects	Headache, sedation, dizziness, postural hypotension, insomnia, agitation/akathisia, EPS, photosensitivity, rash.
Most worrisome adverse effects	NMS, seizures, acute dystonia, tardive dyskinesia, QT prolongation, parkinsonism, priapism, teratogenicity (category C). Endocrine: temp dysregulation. GI: dysphagia.
Initiation/maintenance treatment	**Initial dosage:** 20–40 mg bid. (take med with food) **Maintenance treatment:** 40–80 mg bid. **Sequential care:** 40 mg x bid 1–14; 60 mg x bid 7–21; 80 mg x bid 14–35; titrate to clinical response, not dose or level. **Urgent care:** 40 mg intramuscular or 60–80 mg x bid 1–7; 80–120 mg x bid 3–14; usual effective range 120–160 mg/day.
Laboratories	**Pretreatment:** none required. Useful: weight, glucose, CBC + diff, electrolytes, LFT, EKG, AIMS. **Follow-up:** required: weight. Useful: glucose, CBC + diff, electrolytes, prolactin level, LFT, EKG , discontinue if persistent QTc measurements >500 msec.
Patient education	**Expect** (at least transiently): one or more of: sedation, headache, dry mouth/constipation, tremor/muscle stiffness, lightheadedness. **Report:** severe tremor/rigidity, rash; persistent sore throat/fever, jaundice, akathisia. **Be aware of:** take med with food, drug interactions, potential for diabetes, potential for tardive dyskinesia.

Antidepressants

General antidepressant profiles are shown in Table 8.2 and a comparison of standard antidepressant drugs commonly used for BD is listed below.

Heterocyclics

Significant contraindications	MAO-I in past 2 weeks,NA glaucoma. Cardiac: arrhythmias, conduction defects (>1st degree), tachycardia, post myocardial infarction (acute), seizure disorder, hyperthyroidism, sympathomimetic abuse (cocaine).
Drug interactions	**MAO-I:** hypertensive crisis, sympathomimetic. Antihypertensives: clonidine, guanethidine. **Levels increased by:** SSRIs, neuroleptic, valproate, H2 blockers. **Levels decreased by:** p450 inducers, CBZ, diphenylhydantoin, barbiturates.
Most common adverse effects	Sedation, anticholinergic, hypotension, weight gain. Less common: jitters, sweating, sexual dysfunction.
Most worrisome adverse effects	Mania/hypomania, seizures, serotonin syndrome, allergic, hypertension, arrhythmia.
Laboratories	**Pretreatment:** required: EKG for men >35 and women >40. Useful: CBC, electrolytes, LFT, TFT. **Follow-up:** Useful: EKG, CBC, electrolytes, LFT.
Patient education	**Expect** (at least transiently): one or more of: sedation, dry mouth/constipation, tremor/muscle stiffness, lightheadedness, blurry vision. **Report:** rash, severe headache, severe tremor, jaundice, urinary retention, persistent sore throat/fever, abnormal mood elevation.

					Comparison of Standard Antidepressant Drugs Commonly Used for Bipolar Disorder			
Drug	**Sed**	**AC**	**HypoT**	**SD**	**Advantages**	**Disadvantages**	**USD (mg)**	**UED (mg)**
Imipramine	+++	+++	++	++		Seizure risk 0.1%	25–50 qhs-bid	150–300
Desipramine	-/++	++	+	+	Can be activating	Activation may be excessive, jitters, insomnia	25–50 qam/qhs/bid	150–300
Amitriptyline	+++ +	++++	+++	+++		Sedation, weight gain, hypotension	25–50 qhs-bid	150–300
Nortriptyline	++	++	+	++	Mildly sedating, least hypotension of TCAs	Seizure risk 0.1%	10–25 qhs-bid	75–150
Doxepin	+++ +	+++	++	+++	Sedating, effective antihistamine Effective H2 blocker	Most weight gain	25–50 qhs-bid	150–300
Protriptyline	-/+	+++	++	+	Useful for sleep apnea, most activation of TCAs	Jitters, insomnia, longest half life TCA	5–10 qam-bid	15–60
Fluoxetine	-/+	-	-	+++	Few need >20 mg, activating, very safe in overdose, few experience weight gain	Headache, nausea, rash, jitters, seizure risk 0.2%	10–20 qam	10–60
Sertraline	-/+	-	-	+++	Fewer drug–drug interactions, activating, very safe in overdose, few experience weight gain	Headache, nausea, rash, jitters	50 qam	50–200
Paroxetine	-/++	?/++	-	+++	Short T1/2, no metabolites, jitters less likely, may be less mania	Sedation, anticholinergic-like, drug–drug interactions	20 qam or qhs	20–50
Bupropion	-/+	-	-	-	Activating, few experience weight gain, less therapy-emergent mania, no sexual dysfunction	Seizure risk 0.1% Confusional state	IR 75–100 qam/bid SR/XL 100–150 qam	IR 100 tid 150 bid-tid SR 150–200 bid XL 300–450 qam
Escitalopram	-/+	-	-	+	Few drug–drug interactions, activating, very safe in overdose, few experience weight gain	Nausea, insomnia	10	10–20 qam

Table 8.2. AC, anticholinergic; bid, twice daily; HypoT, hypotension; H2, histamine 2; IR, immediate release; qam, every morning; qhs, every night at bedtime; Sed, sedation; SD, sexual dysfunction; SR, sustained release; TCA, tricyclic antidepressant; tid, three times daily; UED, usual effective dose; USD, usual starting dose; WG, weight gain; XL, extended release; - none/infrequent; +, common; ++, frequent; +++, most frequent; ?, questionable/possible.

126

SSRIs

Significant contraindications	MAO-I in past 6 weeks, hyperthyroidism, sympathomimetic abuse (cocaine).
Drug interactions	**MAO-I:** hypertensive crisis, sympathomimetic. Antihypertensives: clonidine, guanethidine. **Levels increased by:** SSRIs, neuroleptic, valproate, H2 blockers. **Levels decreased by:** p450 inducers, CBZ, diphenylhydantoin, barbiturates. Markedly elevate many drug levels, significant elevation of heterocyclic levels are common (probably greatest with paroxetine).
Most common adverse effects	Most common: headache, nausea, insomnia (difficulty falling asleep), diarrhea, abdominal discomfort, anxiety/jitters, decreased appetite, sexual dysfunction. Less common: agitation, drowsiness, sweating.
Most worrisome adverse effects	Mania/hypomania, seizures, rash, joint pain or swelling.
Laboratories	**Pretreatment:** none required. Useful: CBC, electrolytes, LFT, TFT. **Follow-up:** Useful: EKG, CBC, erythrocyte sedimentation rate, electrolytes, LFT.
Patient education	**Expect** (at least transiently): one or more of: headache, GI side effects (discomfort, nausea, diarrhea), insomnia (difficulty falling asleep), anxiety/jitters, sexual dysfunction. **Report:** rash, severe headache, severe tremor, joint pain/swelling, abnormal mood elevation.

Bupropion

Significant contraindications	Seizure disorder, abnormal electroencephalogram, eating disorders.
Drug interactions	**Levels increased by:** CPY 2B6 inhibitors (orphenadrine, thiopeta, cyclophosphamide). Inhibitor of CPY 2D6. Increases levels of certain antidepressants (eg, imipramine, desipramine, paroxetine, sertraline), antipsychotic drugs (eg haloperidol, risperidone, thioridazine,), beta-blockers (eg, metoprolol), Type 1C antiarrhythmics (eg, propafenone, flecainide).
Most common adverse effects	Most common: nausea, insomnia (difficulty falling asleep), abdominal discomfort, anxiety/jitters, decreased appetite. Less common: diarrhea, agitation.
Most worrisome adverse effects	Seizures.
Laboratories	**Pretreatment:** none required.
Patient education	**Expect** (at least transiently): one or more of: nausea, insomnia (difficulty falling asleep), diarrhea, abdominal discomfort, anxiety/jitters, decreased appetite.

Appendices

Please note: Appendices 1, 2, 4 and 5 are adaptations of tools that are available for clinicians and patients. These are intended as an example; full-size downloadable forms are available from www.manicdepressive.org.

Appendix 1: Clinical Monitoring: Treatment and Symptoms

Name: .... Date: ....

ID#: .... Others: ....

Physician: .... CPT code: ....

Visit Type: ....

Over the past 10 days, how many days have you been/had

	% days	Severity (0–4)	DSM Criteria	DSM Criteria Satisfied No	Probable	Definite
Depressed **most of day**	......	....	Depressed most of the day nearly every day for >2 weeks	☐	☐	☐
Less interest in **most** activities or found you **couldn't enjoy even pleasurable activities** through **most of the day**	......	....	Decreased interest or diminished pleasure in most activities most of the day nearly every day for >2 weeks	☐	☐	☐
Any period of abnormal mood elevation	......	....	Mood elevation (high, euphoric, expansive) to a significant degree over a 4–7 day period	☐	☐	☐
Any period of abnormal irritability	......	....	Irritability to a significant degree over a 4–7 day period	☐	☐	☐
Any abnormal anxiety	......	......				

Rate Associated Symptoms for PAST WEEK

Key:	Much more +2 ———————	Usual/none 0 ———————	Much less −2

MDE	Depression	Sleep	Interest	Guilt/SE	Energy	Conc/Distr	Appetite	PMR/PMA	SI
	....	....	....	....	....	....	....	....	....
				or		or		or	
	....	....	....	....	....	....	....	....	

Requires ⩾5 (including depressed mood and/or interest)

Sleeps .... - .... hours   EMA ....   LNWL ....

EBT ....   DGOOB ....   Passive ....

DFA ....   Naps ....   Active ....

MCA ....   Anhedonia ....

Elevation	Self esteem	Need for sleep	Talking	FOI/Racing thoughts	Distractible	Goal directed activity /PMA	High-risk Behavior
	....	....	....	....	....	....	....
				or		or	
	....	....	....	....	....	....	....

Mania/hypomania requires >3 unless only irritable, then >4 moderate sxs are required
(do not count elevation or irritability) toward dx of hypomania or mania

New major stressor   ☐ Yes   ☐ No
if Yes: ....

Significant medical illness   ☐ Yes   ☐ No
if Yes: ....

c/d caffeine: ....   **Additional** Psych tx: OP   ER   Hosp: ....

ppd nicotine: ....   **Additional** Gen Med tx: OP   ER   Hosp: ....

Alcohol abuse: ☐ Yes   ☐ No   d-use/wk: ....

Substance abuse: ☐ Yes   ☐ No   d/wk: ....

Onset of menses: ....   ☐ early   ☐ late   ☐ NA

Panic attacks: ....   Migraine HA: ....

Binge/purge: ....   weight: ....

HA: ....

Selected Mental Status (Severity 0–4)   OC: ....

PI: ....   Hallucinations: ....

IOR: ....   Delusions: ....

Last Labs   Date: ....

Li: ....   TSH: ....

VPA: ....   Creat: ....

Current Clinical Status   ☐ Continued Sx   ☐ Recovered
(check one)   ☐ Hypomania   ☐ Mixed*
          ☐ Recovering   ☐ Roughening
☐ Depression   ☐ Mania

If new episode, estimate onset date: ....   Other Dx: ....

CGI: ....   GAF: ....   GAF: ....
(1–7 week)   (0–90 month)   (0–90 month)

Current Treatments

Mood stabilizers	Dose mg 24 total	mg missed past 7 days	Dose mg 24 total	mg missed past 7 days
....	....	....	....	....
....	....	....	....	....
....	....	....	....	....
Antidepressants				
....	....	....	....	....
Antipsychotics				
....	....	....	PRN	X ....
....	....	....	PRN	X ....

Adverse Effects

Severity 0–4

Tremor ....
Dry mouth ....
Sedation ....
Constipation ....
Diarrhea ....
Headache ....
Poor memory ....
Sexual dysfunction ....
Increased appetite ....
Other ....
....

Psychosocial Interventions: ..../mo
ECT: ..../mo
Other: ..../mo
Significant Noncompliance: ☐ Yes   ☐ No
if Yes: ....

Path: ....   Phase: A C M T
Path: ....   Phase: A C M T

Comments: ....
....
....
....
....

Plan: ....
....
....

Appendix 2: Mood Chart

Name: .... Date: ....

TREATMENTS (Enter number of tablets taken each day)								
..... mg	Antipsychotic ..... mg	..... mg	Antidepressant ..... mg	Anticonvulsant ..... mg	Benzodiazepine ..... mg	Lithium ..... mg	Verbal Therapy	DAILY NOTES
								Weight

MOOD Rate with 2 marks each day to indicate best and worst

0=none 1=mild 2=moderate 3=severe Irritability	Anxiety	Hours Slept Last Night	Depressed			Circle date to indicate Menses	WNL	Elevated			Psychotic Symptoms Strange Ideas, Hallucinations
			severe	moderate	mild			mild	moderate	severe	
			Significant Impairment NOT ABLE TO WORK	Significant Impairment ABLE TO WORK	Without Significant Impairment		MOOD NOT DEFINITELY ELEVATED OR DEPRESSED. NO SYMPTOMS	Without Significant Impairment	Significant Impairment ABLE TO WORK	Significant Impairment NOT ABLE TO WORK	
						1					
						2					
						3					
						4					
						5					
						6					
						7					
						8					
						9					
						10					
						11					
						12					
						15					
						16					
						17					
						18					
						19					
						20					
						21					
						22					
						23					
						24					
						25					
						26					
						27					
						28					
						29					
						30					
						31					

Appendix 3: Bipolarity Index

For each of the items below circle the item characteristic of the patient
Most convincing characteristic = 20
Convincing characteristic of Bipolar Disorder = 15
Known associated feature of Bipolar Disorder = 10
Nonspecific feature suggestive of Bipolar Disorder = 5
Feature with possible relationship to Bipolar Disorder = 2
No evidence of Bipolar Disorder = 0

	I Episode Characteristics	**Score = ... / 20**
20	Documented acute mania or mixed episode with prominent euphoria, grandiosity or expansiveness and no significant general medical or known secondary etiology	....
15	Clear-cut acute mixed episode or dysphoric, or irritable mania with no significant general medical or known secondary etiology	....
10	Clear-cut hypomania with no significant general medical or known secondary etiology	....
	Clear-cut cyclothymia with no significant general medical or known secondary etiology	....
	Clear-cut mania secondary to antidepressant use	....
5	Clear-cut hypomania secondary to antidepressant use	....
	Episodes with characteristics sxs of hypomania but symptoms, duration or intensity are subthreshold for hypomania or cyclothymia	....
	– A single major depressive episode with psychotic or atypical features (atypical = 2 of 3: hypersomnia, hyperphagia, leaden paralysis of limbs)	....
	– Any postpartum depression	....
2	Any recurrent typical unipolar major depressive disorder	....
	History of any kind of psychotic episode (ie, presence of delusions, hallucinations, ideas of reference, or magical thinking)	....
0	No history of significant mood elevation, recurrent depression, or psychosis	....

	II Age of Onset (1st affective episode/syndrome)	**Score = .../ 20**
20	Age 15–19 yrs	....
15	Age <15 or 20–30	....
10	First episode age 30–45	....
5	First episode >45	....
0	No history of affective illness (no episodes, cyclothymia, dysthymia or BP NOS)	....

	III Course of Illness/Associated Features	**Score = .../20**
20	Recurrent distinct manic episodes separated by periods of full recovery	....
15	– Recurrent distinct manic episodes with incomplete inter-episode recovery	....
	– Recurrent distinct hypomanic episodes with full inter-episode recovery	....
10	– Comorbid substance abuse. Psychotic features only during acute mood episodes	....
	– Incarceration or repeated legal offenses related to manic behavior (eg, shoplifting, reckless driving, bankruptcy)	....
5	– Recurrent unipolar MDD with 3 or more major depressive episodes	....
	– Recurrent distinct hypomanic episodes without full inter-episode recovery	....

    – Recurrent medication noncompliance   ....

    – Comorbid borderline personality   ....

    – Comorbid anxiety or eating disorders (eg, OCD, panic disorder, bulimia)   ....

    – History of ADHD in childhood and periods of above average scholastic or   ....
      social function

    – Gambling, risky investment, overspending, or sexual indiscretions have   ....
      (or would if not concealed) pose a problem for patient, friends, or family

    – Behavioral evidence of perimenstrual exacerbation of mood symptoms   ....

2   – Baseline hyperthymic personality (when not manic or depressed)   ....

    – Married 3 or more times (including remarriage to same individual)   ....

    – In 2 or more years has started a new job and changed jobs after less than year   ....

    – Has more than 2 advanced degrees

0   None of the above   ....

IV   Response to Treatment   Score = .../ 20

20   Full recovery within 4 weeks of therapeutic treatment with mood-stabilizing medication ....

15   Full recovery within 12 weeks of therapeutic treatment with mood-stabilizing   ....
      medication or relapse within 12 weeks of discontinuing treatment

      Affective switch to mania (pure or mixed) within 12 weeks of starting a new   ....
      antidepressant or increasing dose

10   Worsening dysphoria or mixed symptoms during antidepressant treatment   ....
      subthreshold for mania

      Partial response to 1 or 2 mood stabilizers within 12 weeks of therapeutic   ....
      treatment

      Antidepressant-induced new or worsening rapid-cycling course   ....

5   Treatment resistance: lack of response to complete trials of 3 or more antidepressants ....

      Affective switch to mania or hypomania with antidepressant withdrawal   ....

2   Immediate near-complete response to antidepressants (in 1 week or less)   ....

0   None of the above or no treatment   ....

V   Family History   Score = ... / 20

20   At least 1 first-degree relative with documented bipolar illness   ....

15   At least 1 second-degree relative with documented bipolar illness   ....

      At least 1 first-degree relative with documented recurrent unipolar MDD and   ....
      behavioral evidence suggesting bipolar illness

10   First-degree relative with documented recurrent unipolar MDD or schizoaffective disorder ....

      Any relative with documented bipolar illness. Any relative with documented recurrent ....
      unipolar MDD and behavioral evidence suggesting bipolar illness

5   First-degree relative with documented substance abuse or any relative with possible   ....
      bipolar illness

2   First-degree relative with possible recurrent unipolar MDD   ....

      First-degree relative with diagnosed related illness: anxiety disorders, eating disorders, ADD............

0   None of the above or no family psychiatric illness   ....

Total Score   ..../ 100

Appendix 4: Waiting Room Clinical Self-Report Form

Name: .... Date: ....

Clinician: .... ID#: ....

Since your last appointment:	Yes	No
Has there been a period of time when you were feeling down or depressed most of the day, nearly everyday?	☐	☐
If Yes, did it last as long as 2 weeks?	☐	☐
What about being a lot less interested in most things or unable to enjoy things you usually enjoy?	☐	☐
If Yes, did it last as long as 2 weeks?	☐	☐
Has there been a period of time when you were feeling so good or so hyper people thought you were not your normal self or you were so hyper you got in trouble?	☐	☐
If Yes, was it more than just feeling good?	☐	☐
Did anyone say you were manic?	☐	☐
What about a period of time when you were so irritable that you would shout at people or start fights or arguments?	☐	☐
Have you experienced a major stress that you feel has caused your mood to change?	☐	☐
if Yes (describe)		
Have you experienced other medical problems?	☐	☐
if Yes (describe)		
Used additional psychiatric care/treatment	☐	☐
Other medical treatment	☐	☐
Onset of last menses		

Over the past 10 days how many days have you been/had:

depressed most of the day	........./10 days	any period of abnormal irritability	........./10 days
unable to experience pleasure most of the day	........./10 days	any period of abnormal anxiety	........./10 days
any period of abnormal mood elevation	........./10 days		

During the past week:

What is the least you have slept in any 1 day	.... hrs	What is the most you have slept any 1 day	.... hrs

Have you had:	Yes	No		Yes	No
Panic attacks	☐	☐	Headaches	☐	☐
Binge/purge	☐	☐	Weight:		

Indicate your use of:

Caffeine	cups/day	Alcohol	drinks/week
Nicotine	packs/day	Drugs	

For each item, rate this week compared to your usual (when well)	Decreased				Well		Increased			
	Constant and severe	Nearly every Day	Often	Rarely and/or mild	**Normal**	Rarely and/or mild	Often	Nearly every day	Constant and severe	
Sleep	☐	☐	☐	☐	☐	■	☐	☐	☐	☐
Ability to enjoy pleasant things/usual interests	☐	☐	☐	☐	☐	■	☐	☐	☐	☐
Self confidence/self esteem	☐	☐	☐	☐	☐	■	☐	☐	☐	☐
Energy	☐	☐	☐	☐	☐	■	☐	☐	☐	☐
Ability to concentrate	☐	☐	☐	☐	☐	■	☐	☐	☐	☐
Distractibility	☐	☐	☐	☐	☐	■	☐	☐	☐	☐
Appetite	☐	☐	☐	☐	☐	■	☐	☐	☐	☐
Physical restlessness/agitation	☐	☐	☐	☐	☐	■	☐	☐	☐	☐
Rate of speech or thoughts	☐	☐	☐	☐	☐	■	☐	☐	☐	☐
Feel life isn't worth living or suicidal thoughts	☐	☐	☐	☐	☐	■	☐	☐	☐	☐
Talking	☐	☐	☐	☐	☐	■	☐	☐	☐	☐
Racing thoughts	☐	☐	☐	☐	☐	■	☐	☐	☐	☐
Making plans or getting new projects started	☐	☐	☐	☐	☐	■	☐	☐	☐	☐
Behaviors others regard as excessive, foolish, or risky	☐	☐	☐	☐	☐	■	☐	☐	☐	☐

Please complete for all medications used since your last visit

Medication	Total daily dose	mg missed this week	Comments/ adverse effects	Check if no adverse effects

Appendix 5: Collaborative Care Plan: Treatment Contract

The purpose of this contract is to organize my care for bipolar disorder, with attention to both the prevention of mood episodes and the efficient treatment of these episodes should they occur.

My first step in guiding my care is the selection of my support team. The team members should include people with whom I have regular contact, who can help me identify episodes should they occur and help me put into practice some of the strategies and plans I choose to control my illness.

(Select your treatment support team including key care providers and other supports; for example, you may select your psychiatrist, psychologist, social worker, and other team members drawn from your support network.)

Treatment Contract – Support Team

Role/relationship	Name	Contact information
My Psychiatrist	....	Phone: ....
My Therapist	....	Phone: ....
My Primary Care Provider	....	Phone: ....
	....	Phone: ....
	....	Phone: ....
	....	Phone: ....

When I am well I:

- ☐ Keep a regular sleep schedule (usually .... to .... hours/night)
- ☐ Arrive on time for work and/or school
- ☐ Take all medications as prescribed by my doctor
- ☐ Maintain regular appointments with my psychiatrist at ..../month
- ☐ Maintain regular appointments with my therapist at ..../month
- ☐ Maintain my grooming
- ☐ Maintain a schedule including at least .... valued activities each day as a buffer against stress
- ☐ Avoid excessive use of alcohol
- ☐ Avoid all use of illicit drugs
- ☐ Keep a perspective on my thoughts, and evaluate my thoughts for accuracy
- ☐ Share with my family information on communication styles that may reduced stress
- ☐ Other ....
- ☐ Other ....
- ☐ Other ....
- ☐ Other ....

My second step is to identify the plans I will use to help control my bipolar disorder so that I can best pursue my life goals.

My goal now is to identify some of the strategies and tools I will use and that I want my team to use.

Check Intent to Use

☐ Monitor my mood for early intervention
I am aware of the signs of depression and mania (available from my care provider). In addition to these symptoms, I know from my own patterns that I should watch out for the following signs:

  ☐ Depressed thoughts ....
  ☐ Depressed symptoms ....
  ☐ Depressed behaviors ....
  ☐ Hypomanic thoughts ....
  ☐ Hypomanic symptoms ....
  ☐ Hypomanic behaviors ....

☐ Take early action if I notice signs of depression or mania
  ☐ Contact my psychiatrist at phone # ....
  ☐ Contact my therapist at phone # ....
  ☐ Contact my support person at phone # ....
  ☐ Maintain a regular schedule of sleep and activities
  ☐ Maintain a regular schedule of pleasant events
  ☐ Evaluate my thoughts for negative or hyperpositive thinking
  ☐ Talk with my family about ways to cope
  ☐ Limit my alcohol use and avoid all non-medication drugs
  ☐ Other ....
  ☐ Other ....
  Other ....
  Other ....

☐ Contact the following people should I ever have strong suicidal thoughts:
  ☐ Contact my psychiatrist at phone # ....
  ☐ Contact my therapist at phone # ....
  ☐ Contact my support person at phone # ....
  ☐ Other action ....

☐ Keep myself safe until I can be seen or go to a local emergency room if I ever fear I may act on suicidal thoughts

☐ If I start to become depressed, I would like my support team to:
  ☐ Talk to me about my symptoms (who ....)
  ☐ Make plans for a pleasant event (who ....)
  ☐ Encourage me to participate when I am pessimistic (who ....)
  ☐ Discuss ways to reduce stress (who ....)
  ☐ Make sure I am taking my medication (who ....)
  ☐ Make sure I notify work and/or school (who ....)
  ☐ Call my doctor if I am unable to (who ....)
  ☐ Other ....

☐ Other ....

☐ Other ....

☐ If I start to become manic, I would like my support team to:

    ☐ Talk to me about my symptoms (who ....)

    ☐ Talk to me about reducing activities (who ....)

    ☐ Talk to me about neutral subjects only (who ....)

    ☐ Allow me to be alone if I am irritable (who ....)

    ☐ Ignore my sarcastic comments (who ....)

    ☐ Make sure I take my medication (who ....)

    ☐ Take care of the kids/pets/other (who ....)

    ☐ Take away my credit cards (who ....)

    ☐ Take away my car keys (who ....)

    ☐ Take me to the hospital (preferred hospital ....)

    ☐ Other ....

    ☐ Other ....

    ☐ Other ....

I designed this contract so that I can take an active role in my treatment. My goal is to maximize my control by arranging for my treatment team to take care of me when I may be unable to follow this plan myself. So that any future decisions are well considered, I agree to change this contract only after giving two weeks' written notice to all the parties to this contract.

Signatures of contracting individuals

Signature: .... Date: ....

Signature: .... Date: ....

Signature: .... Date: ....

Signature: .... Date: ....

Resources for patients

Support Advocacy/Consumer Organizations

Argentina

Asociación Argentina de Psiquiatría Biológica (AAPB) www.aapb.org.ar

Australia

SANE Australia www.sane.org

Brazil

ABRATA: Associação Brasileira de Familiares, Amigos e Portadores, de Transtornos Afetivos www.abrata.com.br

Canada

Canadian Mental Health Association – Calgary Region www.cmha-ascr.ab.ca
Center for Suicide Prevention www.suicideinfo.ca

Germany

German Bipolar Disorder Society (DGBS e.V.) www.dgbs.de/dgbs/index.php

Verein Horizonte e.V. www.verein-horizonte.de
Verein zur Förderung affektiv Erkrankter
Hotline: 0700 5522 8822

Norway

Bipolar Research and Innovation Network www.norbrain.no
Norsk selskap for bipolare lidelser www.bipolardisorder.no
Norwegian Medical Association: www.legeforeningen.no
Norwegian Psychiatry Association www.psykiatri.no

United Kingdom

Manic Depression Fellowship www.mdf.org.uk/bipolar

Mind www.mind.org.uk

Depression Alliance www.depressionalliance.org

United States

Child & Adolescent Bipolar Foundation www.bpkids.org

Depression and Bipolar Support Alliance www.dbsalliance.org

National Alliance for the Mentally Ill www.nami.org

National Mental Health Association www.nmha.org

Anxiety Disorders Association of America www.adaa.org

American Foundation for Suicide Prevention www.afsp.org

Families for Depression Awareness www.familyaware.org

McMan's Depression and Bipolar Web www.mcmanweb.com/articles.htm

Massachusetts General Hospital

Mood and Anxiety Disorders Institute www.mghmadi.org

The Depression Clinical and Research Program www.mghdepression.org

Harvard Bipolar Research Program www.manicdepressive.org

The Center for Anxiety and Traumatic Stress Related Disorder
www.mghanxiety.org

Center for Women's Mental Health
www.womensmentalhealth.org/resources/clinical.html

Child & Adolescent Psychiatry
www.massgeneral.org/allpsych/mgh_Psychiatry_pediatric.htm

ARCH – Access to Resources for Community Health (An electronic health information and resource center that provides information to the public. Covers mental health as well as all health issues.) www.mgh.harvard.edu/library/arch/arch.asp

Other Useful Websites

Medical Information

National Institute of Mental Health www.nimh.nih.gov

Bipolar Disorder Information Booklet
www.nimh.nih.gov/publicat/bipolarmenu.cfm

US Food and Drug Administration – Consumer Drug Information
www.fda.gov/cder/consumerinfo

Physician's Desk Reference www.pdr.net/pdrnet/librarian

National Library of Medicine MEDLINEplus www.nlm.nih.gov/medlineplus

PubMed www.ncbi.nlm.nih.gov/pubmed

Massachusetts Department of Mental Health www.state.ma.us/dmh

STEP-BD Homepage: www.stepbd.org

Books and Articles

For a person or family living with a mood or anxiety disorder, information in books and articles can be a gateway to better understanding and comfort.

Books and Other Resources

The Bipolar Disorder Survival Guide: What You and Your Family Need to Know by David J Miklowitz

An Unquiet Mind: A Memoir of Moods and Madness by Kay Redfield Jamison

Surviving Manic Depression: A Manual on Bipolar Disorder for Patients, Families, and Providers by E Fuller Torrey, Michael B Knable

Brilliant Madness: Living with Manic Depressive Illness by Gloria Hochman (Contributor), Patty Duke (Author)

Electroboy: A Memoir of Mania by Andy Behrman

Darkness Visible: A Memoir of Madness by William Styron

Postcards From the Edge by Carrie Fisher

Survival Strategies for Parenting Children with Bipolar Disorder: Innovative parenting and counseling techniques for helping children with bipolar disorder and the conditions that may occur with it by George T Lynn

Living Without Depression and Manic Depression: A Workbook for Maintaining Mood Stability by Mary Ellen Copeland

Manic-Depressive Illness by Frederick K. Goodwin M.D., Kay Redfield Jamison

Bipolar Disorder: Rebuilding Your Life by James T Stout

The British National Formulary (BNF). British Medical Association and the Royal Pharmaceutical Society of Great Britain, 1998. The standard reference for prescribing and dispensing drugs in the UK, updated twice yearly.

John D Preston, John H O'Neal, and Mary C Talaga. Consumer's Guide to Psychiatric Drugs. Oakland, California: New Harbinger Publications, 1998.

Harold M Silverman, editor. The Pill Book, 8th ed. New York: Bantam Books, 1998. A basic paperback guide to the most commonly used medications in the US.

Donald Sullivan. The American Pharmaceutical Association's Guide to Prescription Drugs. New York: Signet, 1998.

Timothy E Wilens, MD. Straight Talk About Psychiatric Medications for Kids. New York: Guilford Press, 1998.

How to Find...

When a person or family is coping with mental illness, particularly during an acute crisis, one of the biggest challenges is to find appropriate resources for getting help. To follow is a list of some of the resources that may be useful for helping you or a loved one cope with mental illness.

Find a Mental Health Facility

US Department of Health and Human Services – Substance Abuse and Mental Health Services Administration (SAMHSA): National Mental Health Information Center
www.mentalhealth.org/databases/MHDMappoint.asp?D1=MA&Type=MHDR
SAMHSA lists mental health facilities in the Commonwealth of Massachusetts.

New England Psychologist 781-237-9909 www.nepsy.com
New England Psychologist, a monthly print publication for licensed psychologists in the region, compiles a directory of psychiatric hospitals in New England from information provided by hospitals in response to a questionnaire.

Find a Referral

Best Doctors, Inc. 888-362-8677 www.bestdoctors.com
Two fee-based services are offered. "Internet Subscription" allows you to search for a psychiatrist in your geographic area. "FindBestDoc" is a personalized service that provides you with the names of three physicians in your area whose availability to see new patients has been confirmed.

American Medical Association (AMA) 312-464-5000 www.ama-assn.org
AMA Doctor Finder provides basic professional information about licensed psychiatrists in the United States.

American Psychological Association (APA) Referral Line 800-964-2000
www.apa.org
The APA can help you locate a licensed psychologist in your area.

National Association of Social Workers – Massachusetts Chapter (NASW–MA)
www.naswma.org

Social Work Therapy Referral Service 617-720-2828 or 800-242-9794

NASW-MA offers free telephone referral services for individual, couple, and family therapy, as well as group therapy referrals.

Find Respite Care

The ARCH National Respite Locator Service 800-473-1727 www.respitelocator.org This organization helps parents, caregivers, and professionals find respite care in their state and local areas. Respite care allows family members to get a break from caring for an ill family member.

Find State and Local Services

US Department of Health and Human Services – Substance Abuse and Mental Health Services Administration (SAMHSA): National Mental Health Information Center www.mentalhealth.org/publications/allpubs/stateresourceguides/Massachusetts01.a sp SAMHSA lists a variety of state and local mental health resources.

On-line

On-line counseling is available at the following addresses and sites:

www.befrienders.org/email.html
– a 24-hour confidential e-mail service by the Samaritans.

www.kidshelp.sympatico.ca
– a service for young people – also addresses issues other than suicide.

National Crisis Helpline – for use in locating the nearest crisis service in the United States. Phone Toll Free 1-800-999-9999.

www.metanoia.org/suicide
– contains conversations and writings for suicidal persons to read. If you're feeling at all suicidal, be sure to read this page before you take any action. It might just save your life.

San Francisco Suicide Prevention (SFSP) – services are provided 24 hours a day by over 250 trained volunteers. Basic information on suicide (warning signs, advice, statistics and more) is also featured.

Crisis Support Services of Alameda County, California – services provided include 24-hour telephone counseling, grief counseling, stress counseling, community education program, seniors program.

Boys Town National Crisis Line – 24 hours a day, every day: the only national crisis line that children and parents can call with any problem, any time. The hotline is staffed by caring professionals. Phone Toll Free 1-800-448-3000, or for TDD call 800-448-1833.